SEP   2005

Cooking Around The World

MEXICAN

70 SPICY AND SIZZLING RECIPES FROM SOUTH OF THE BORDER

Elisabeth Lambert Ortiz

LORENZ BOOKS

This edition is published by Lorenz Books

Lorenz Books is an imprint of Anness Publishing Ltd
Hermes House, 88–89 Blackfriars Road, London SE1 8HA
tel. 020 7401 2077; fax 020 7633 9499
www.lorenzbooks.com; info@anness.com

© Anness Publishing Ltd 1996, 2004

UK agent: The Manning Partnership Ltd,
6 The Old Dairy, Melcombe Road, Bath BA2 3LR;
tel. 01225 478444; fax 01225 478440; sales@manning-partnership.co.uk

UK distributor: Grantham Book Services Ltd,
Isaac Newton Way, Alma Park Industrial Estate, Grantham, Lincs NG31 9SD;
tel. 01476 541080; fax 01476 541061; orders@gbs.tbs-ltd.co.uk

North American agent/distributor: National Book Network,
4501 Forbes Boulevard, Suite 200, Lanham, MD 20706;
tel. 301 459 3366; fax 301 429 5746; www.nbnbooks.com

Australian agent/distributor: Pan Macmillan Australia,
Level 18, St Martins Tower, 31 Market St, Sydney, NSW 2000;
tel. 1300 135 113; fax 1300 135 103; customer.service@macmillan.com.au

New Zealand agent/distributor: David Bateman Ltd,
30 Tarndale Grove, Off Bush Road, Albany, Auckland;
tel. (09) 415 7664; fax (09) 415 8892

Publisher: Joanna Lorenz
Senior Cookery Editor: Linda Fraser
Copy Editor: Jenni Fleetwood
Designer: Siân Keogh
Photography: David Jordan
Food for photography and styling: Judy Williams, assisted by Manisha Kanani
Illustrator: Madeleine David

Previously published as *Creative Cooking Library: Taste of Mexico*

1 3 5 7 9 10 8 6 4 2

Notes
For all recipes, quantities are given in both metric and imperial measures and, where appropriate,
measures are also given in standard cups and spoons. Follow one set, but not a mixture because
they are not interchangeable.

Standard spoon and cup measurements are level.
1 tsp = 5ml, 1 tbsp = 15ml, 1 cup = 250ml/8fl oz

Australian standard tablespoons are 20ml. Australian readers should use 3 tsp in place of 1 tbsp for
measuring small quantities of gelatine, cornflour, salt etc.

Size 3 (medium) eggs should be used unless otherwise stated.

CONTENTS

INTRODUCTION

Many of the foods we take for granted in the West were unknown before Christopher Columbus reached the Americas in 1492. The list is impressive. We had no corn (maize), tomatoes or peppers (sweet, pungent and hot); no common beans like red kidney or pinto beans, no pumpkins nor any other winter squashes. Courgettes and chayotes (chocho) were equally unfamiliar, as were avocados and guavas, and we had never tasted chocolate or vanilla. Even turkeys were unknown. All these foods originated in Mexico, where agriculture is believed to have practised as long ago as 7000 BC, about the same time, give or take a century or two, as the cultivation of food crops agriculture began in the Middle East.

After the Conquest of Mexico by Hernán Cortés, the Spanish introduced wheat and domesticated animals, hitherto unknown in the Americas. Cattle yielded beef, milk, butter, cream and cheese. The domestic pig, being better to eat, soon ousted the local wild and wily boar and lambs; goats and the domestic hen made their appearance. The Spanish planted olive trees for olive oil and walnut trees, as well as the vegetables that reminded them of home. It was out of this meeting of Old and New Worlds that the cuisine of Mexico developed. This colonial kitchen still rests firmly on its Aztec and Mayan foundations and though it is unique in the world of cooking, it is neither difficult nor inaccessible.

There are no difficult or complicated techniques to master and the unique flavours of Mexican dishes appeal to nearly everyone.

When the Spanish priest, Father Bernadinho Sahagun, visited Mexico at the beginning of the conquest (from 1519–21) he was deeply impressed by the great central market in the Aztec capital. He wrote about the foods he found there, describing the various types of unleavened flat pancakes made from corn (maize) flour which the Spanish called *tortillas*. This bread has the distinction of being made from cooked flour. Dried corn kernels are cooked in water with lime until soft, when the skins can be rubbed off. The corn is drained and ground to a heavy paste. It is sold at the markets to make tortillas, or dried and packaged as *masa harina*, literally "dough flour". Tortillas are easy enough to make at home using a tortilla press, which consists of two hinged circles of wood or metal. A ball of dough is placed on the bottom circle, then the top brought down, flattening it to a round, which is then baked for a minute or two on a *comal*

The varied terrains of Mexico provide a diverse harvest: seafood from the coast, beef from the north and corn from the central plateau.

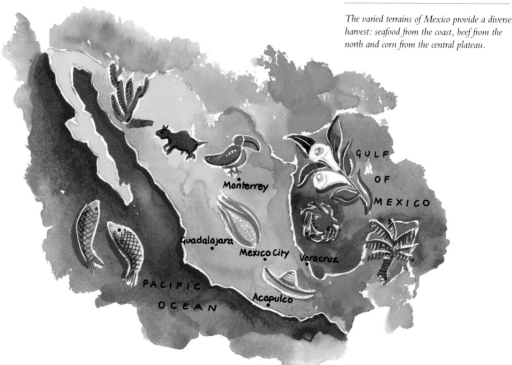

GULF

OF

MEXICO

Monterrey

Guadalajara

Mexico City

Veracruz

Acapulco

PACIFIC

OCEAN

or a griddle. Although many Mexican women still make tortillas at home, some using the ancient skill of patting them out by hand, they can also be purchased uncooked or freshly-baked from *tortillerias*. Tortillas are also exported; you can now buy packets in most supermarkets. They are used as the basis of a number of dishes that the Spanish call *Antojitos*. More than just snack foods or starters, these little whims or fancies form a whole category in the Mexican kitchen.

Of equal importance in Mexican cooking is the family of cultivated capsicums that the Aztecs collectively called chilli, although we tend to differentiate between chillies and the mild-flavoured red, yellow and green peppers. It is estimated there may be over a hundred varieties of chillies, some sold fresh, others pickled or dried. Chillies can irritate delicate skin and it is vital to wash your hands in warm soapy water immediately after handling them. Cooks with particularly sensitive skin should wear gloves.

The tomato is another ingredient essential to Mexican cooking, whether raw or cooked. There is another Mexican tomato, the green husk tomato (*Physalis ixocarpa*) which has an exquisite flavour. It is widely used in Mexico but has never been as popular elsewhere as the red, true tomato, except in Guatemala.

The Mexican kitchen is strongly regional. The cattle country of the north, bordering on Texas, is not good corn country and here the wheat flour tortilla is popular. It is always eaten with roast kid (baby goat), a northern favourite, and *salsa verde* made with the green husk tomato.

Much of the country is at altitudes of 7–8000 feet. Here the climate is temperate and all manner of fruits and vegetables flourish on the high plateau. The town of Puebla is famous for exquisite crystallized fruits including small, juicy and delicious peaches. Puebla is also the home of that great

The unique blend of Old and New World customs, produce and lifestyles is evident in this colourful Oaxaca street scene.

festival dish, *Mole Poblano de Guajolote*. The flavours in the sauce blend well in the long cooking time dictated by the high altitude.

The semi-tropical regions at sea level have abundant tropical fruits and vegetables, including pawpaws (papayas), pineapples and coconuts. The extensive coastline yields a rich harvest of fish and shellfish. Before the Aztecs dominated the country, the Mayan Empire had flourished, invading Mexico's Yucatán peninsula and the southern part of the country. Here the cooking is subtly different. There are many regional chillies as well as unique herbs and spices. *Achiote* (annatto) is especially popular. The area boasts a sauce, *Ixni-pec* (pronounced Schnee-peck), made with the *habanero* chilli – the hottest chilli in North America.

The ancient art of cooking in an earth oven still flourishes in Mexico. For *barbacoa* in the plateau a pit is lined with the leaves of the agave plant. Heated stones are placed in the pit, the food (a whole lamb, vegetables and so on) is arranged on top and the pit is then sealed and the food left to cook.

The agave gives a subtle flavour of tequila to the foods. In Yucatán the earth oven is called a *pib*. It is lined with banana leaves and the meat, a suckling pig or maybe a chicken, is seasoned with achiote among other flavourings, and sprinkled with Seville orange juice, before being sealed in the pit and cooked.

In spite of industrialisation, most people in Mexico prefer to eat their main meal, *comida*, in the middle of the day. This is a long, late lunch, often followed by a siesta. Soup is a must and so are beans. A small dish of beans (usually red kidney or pinto) are served separately after the main course and before dessert, which is often just fresh fruit. Breakfast is coffee with milk and a sweet bread. *Almuerzo*, a light meal which often bridges the gap between breakfast and *comida* usually consists of a corn-based dish and although there may be a proper dinner, *cena*, served very late, more often the last meal is a light supper, *merienda*. This is often comprised of tamales and atole (corn gruel) with perhaps the addition of some sweet breads and jam.

INGREDIENTS

ACHIOTE (ANNATTO)
Prized for its flavouring and colouring qualities, this comes from the hard orange-red coating around the seeds of a small tropical American flowering tree, *Bixa orellana*. The pulp, dissolved in oil or water, imparts a delicate flavour and a deep, golden-orange colour. The small seeds are ground for use as a flavouring.

AVOCADOS
The avocado, which is now grown all over the world, originated in Central America. It was named from the Aztec word *ahuacatl*, which the Spanish called called *aguacate*. There are nearly 500 varieties, but only three distinct types; the Mexican avocado has a thin skin, small fruits, anise-scented leaves and a high oil content.

BEANS
Dried beans (*frijoles*) are a staple in the Mexican diet, either served with a little of the cooking liquid, or mashed and fried with lard or oil as refritos. Pink, red and black haricot beans are native to Mexico, as are speckled pinto beans. Also popular are lima beans from Peru, and garbanzos (also known as chick-peas) which come from the Middle East. In addition there are *ejotes* which are fresh green beans.

Clockwise from top left: dried chick peas, dried kidney beans, fresh green beans and dried pinto beans.

Clockwise from top left: small green chillies, chipotle chillies, mulato chillies, habanero chillies, pasilla chillies, green peppers, green jalapeño chillies, anaheim chillies, and (centre left) Scotch Bonnet chillies, (centre right) fresh red chillies.

CHILLIES AND PEPPERS
These are indigenous to Mexico and there are innumerable varieties. The most commonly used fresh green chillies are *serrano, jalapeño* and *poblano,* all hot. The *habanero* (Scotch Bonnet) is small, flavourful and the hottest chilli in North America. It may be red or green and is used fresh. The most popular dried chillies are *ancho* (full-flavoured and mild) and *chipotle* (very hot). Other varieties include the *mulato,* which is pungent and the hot *pasilla*. In addition there are the bell-shaped so-called sweet peppers or capsicums. These may be green, yellow or red, depending on their ripeness, and they are not hot. Canned or bottled red peppers are called pimientos.

CHAYOTE (CHRISTOPHINE OR CHOCHO)
A small squash indigenous to Mexico, chayotes are round or pear-shaped, light green in colour and may be smooth or corrugated. Delicately flavoured, they have a firm, crisp flesh and large edible seed. They are used as a vegetable accompaniment or in soups or salads.

CHOCOLATE
Chocolate originated in Mexico thousands of years ago. It was drunk as a hot or cold, foam-topped flavoured drink. Today Mexican chocolate is sold in blocks flavoured with cinnamon, almonds and vanilla and is used in drinks and cooking.

CHORIZO
A highly seasoned, reddish-coloured link sausage which is used a great deal in Mexican cooking. It comes in many varieties, but all have pork and paprika in common which gives them their distinctive colour. Some varieties are hotter than others.

CORIANDER (CILANTRO)
This fresh green feathery herb resembles Italian parsley or chervil in appearance and is widely used in Mexican cooking. It is an essential ingredient of guacamole. The seeds are also used, but less extensively.

CORN (MAIZE)
Corn was one of the first plants cultivated in Mexico and is extremely important. The dried kernels are ground to make *masa harina* (literally dough flour), which is used to make tortillas, tamales and a host of other small baked goods, and the drink *atole*.

Clockwise from top left: mint, coriander, flat leaf parsley, oregano and bay leaves.

Clockwise from top left: avocados, string of garlic, chayotes, garlic bulb, tomatoes, onions, tomatillos and canned jalapeño *chillies (in bowl), courgettes, lemons, and lime halves (centre).*

known as "husk tomatoes" because of their papery covering. To date, they are not sold fresh here, but are available in cans from speciality shops. Tomatillos have an exquisite and distinctive flavour and are used in sauces and in the "green" dishes. They have to be cooked for a few minutes to allow their full flavour to develop.

CORN DISHES (ANTOJITOS)
Corn plays a very important role in the Mexican kitchen and is central to the dishes the Spanish dubbed *Antojitos* (little whims or fancies), which are eaten as snacks or light lunches. Some, like tacos, are very simple; others, such as enchiladas, are more elaborate. Tamales consist of steamed dried corn husks or banana leaves with a dough and meat filling. All these dishes are based on *masa harina*, flour made from dried corn boiled in lime water before being ground.

GUACAMOLE
There are many recipes for this classic salsa. In its simplest form it is made by mashing avocados with a squeeze or two of lemon or lime juice, a handful of chopped fresh coriander, a little crushed garlic, chopped spring onions, salt, and chopped fresh serrano chillies.

Clockwise from top left: pumpkin seeds, star anise, masa harina, *plain flour, cinnamon sticks, Mexican chocolate and almonds.*

FLOR DE JAMAICA (ROSELLA OR SORREL)
This is a tropical plant grown for its fleshy red sepals, which are used to make a soft drink in Mexico called Aqua de Jamaica (Jamaica Water).

NOPALES NOPALITOS (PRICKLY PEAR CACTUS PADDLES)
These are the paddles of the prickly pear cactus. The prickly pear can be either red or yellow in colour and is covered in thorns.The cactus paddles are removed and then cleaned before being diced and either canned or bottled. In the Mexican kitchen they are used as a vegetable, in salads, soups and omelettes. The plant bears delicious fruit called "tunas" which are sold fresh in Mexican markets.

PILONCILLO (MEXICAN SUGAR)
This unrefined dark brown cane sugar is sold in cone-shaped loaves. It tastes like molasses and is used to sweeten desserts and coffee. Soft dark brown sugar is a good substitute.

PEPITAS (DRIED PUMPKIN SEEDS)
These are small, plump, delicately-flavoured seeds. Buy the hulled pumpkin seeds that are available in health food shops and delicatessens. Ground to a powder, the seeds are used to flavour and thicken sauces.

TOMATILLOS (MEXICAN GREEN TOMATOES)
These are not unripe ordinary tomatoes but come from a different plant, *Physalis ixocarpa*. They are sometimes

CORN DISHES

*Corn plays a very important role in the Mexican
kitchen and is central to the dishes the Spanish
dubbed Antojitos (little whims or fancies), which
are eaten as snacks or light lunches. Some, like
tacos, are very simple; others, such as enchiladas,
are more elaborate. Tamales consist of steamed
dried corn husks or banana leaves with a dough
and meat filling. All these dishes are based on*
masa harina, *flour made from dried corn boiled in
lime water before being ground.*

Corn Tortillas

Have ready a tortilla press and a small plastic bag, cut open and halved crossways.

INGREDIENTS

Makes about 14 x 14cm/5¹/₂in tortillas
275g/10oz/2 cups *masa harina*
   (tortilla flour)
250–350ml/8–12fl oz/
   1–1¹/₂ cups water

COOK'S TIP

Tortillas are very easy to make but it is important to get the dough texture right. If it is too dry and crumbly, add a little water; if it is too wet, add more *masa harina*. If you misjudge the pressure needed for flattening the ball of dough to a neat circle on the tortilla press, just scrape it off, re-roll it and try again.

1 Put the *masa harina* into a bowl and stir in 250ml/8fl oz/1 cup of the water, mixing to a soft dough that just holds together. If it is too dry, add a little more water. Cover the bowl with a cloth and set aside for 15 minutes.

2 Preheat the oven to 150°C/300°F/ Gas 2. Open the tortilla press and line both sides with the prepared plastic sheets. Preheat a griddle until hot.

3 Knead the dough lightly and shape into 14 balls. Put a ball on the press and bring the top down firmly to flatten the dough out into a round.

4 Open the press. Peel off the top layer of plastic and lift the tortilla by means of the bottom plastic. Turn it on to your palm, so that the plastic is uppermost. Peel off the plastic and flip the tortilla on to the hot griddle.

5 Cook for about 1 minute or until the edges start to curl. Turn over and cook for a further 1 minute. Wrap in foil and keep warm in the oven.

Flour Tortillas

INGREDIENTS

Makes about 14 x 15cm/6in tortillas
225g/8oz/2 cups plain flour
5ml/1 tsp salt
15ml/1 tbsp lard or vegetable fat
120ml/4fl oz/½ cup water

1 Sift the flour and salt into a mixing bowl. Rub in the lard or vegetable fat with your fingertips until the mixture resembles coarse breadcrumbs.

2 Gradually add the water and mix to a soft dough. Knead lightly, form into a ball, cover the bowl with a cloth and leave to rest for 15 minutes.

3 Divide the dough into about 14 portions and form into balls. Roll out each ball of dough in turn on a lightly floured board to a round measuring about 15cm/6in. Trim the rounds if necessary.

COOK'S TIP

Make flour tortillas whenever *masa harina* is hard to find. To keep them soft and pliable, make sure they are kept warm.

4 Heat a medium, ungreased griddle or heavy-based frying pan over a moderate heat. Cook the tortillas, one at a time, for about 1½–2 minutes on each side. Turn over with a large palette knife when the bottom becomes a delicate brown. Adjust the heat if the tortilla browns too quickly.

5 Stack the tortillas in a clean cloth if eating right away. Otherwise wrap in foil and keep warm in the oven.

Mixed Tostadas

Like little edible plates, these fried tortillas can support anything that is not too juicy.

INGREDIENTS

Makes 14
oil, for shallow frying
14 freshly prepared unbaked
  corn tortillas
225g/8oz/1 cup mashed red kidney or
  pinto beans
1 iceberg lettuce, shredded
oil and vinegar dressing (optional)
2 cooked chicken breasts, skinned and
  thinly sliced
225g/8oz Guacamole
115g/4oz/1 cup coarsely grated
  Cheddar cheese
pickled *jalapeño* chillies, seeded and
  sliced, to taste

1 Heat the oil in a frying pan and fry the tortillas until golden brown on both sides and crisp but not hard.

2 Spread each tortilla with a layer of beans. Put a layer of shredded lettuce (which can be left plain or lightly tossed with a little dressing) over the beans.

3 Arrange pieces of chicken in a layer on top of the lettuce. Carefully spread over a layer of the Guacamole and finally sprinkle over a layer of the grated cheese.

4 Arrange the mixed tostadas on a large platter. Serve on individual plates but eat using your hands.

Quesadillas

These delicious filled and deep-fried tortilla turnovers make a popular snack and smaller versions make excellent canapés.

INGREDIENTS

Makes 14
14 freshly prepared unbaked tortillas

For the filling
225g/8oz/1 cup finely chopped or
  grated Cheddar cheese
3 *jalapeño* chillies, seeded and cut
  into strips
salt
oil, for shallow frying

1 Have the tortillas ready, covered with a clean cloth. Combine the grated cheese and chilli strips in a bowl. Season with salt. Set aside.

2 Heat the oil in a frying pan, then holding an unbaked tortilla on your palm, put a spoonful of filling along the centre, avoiding the edges.

--- COOK'S TIP ---

For other stuffing ideas try leftover beans with chillies, or chopped chorizo sausage fried with a little chopped onion.

3 Fold the tortilla and seal the edges by pressing or crimping well together. Fry in hot oil, on both sides, until golden brown and crisp.

4 Using a fish slice, lift out the quesadilla and drain it on kitchen paper. Transfer to a plate and keep warm while frying the remaining quesadillas. Serve hot.

Tortilla Flutes

Flutes or *flautas* look as good as they taste.

INGREDIENTS

Makes about 12

24 freshly prepared unbaked
    flour tortillas
2 tomatoes, peeled, seeded
    and chopped
1 small onion, chopped
1 garlic clove, chopped
30–45ml/2–3 tbsp corn oil
2 freshly cooked chicken breasts,
    skinned and shredded
salt

To garnish
sliced radishes
stuffed green olives

1 Place the unbaked flour tortillas in pairs on a work surface, with the right-hand tortilla overlapping its partner by about 5cm/2in.

2 Put the tomatoes, onion, and garlic into a food processor and process to a purée. Season with salt to taste.

3 Heat 15ml/1 tbsp of the oil in a frying pan and cook the tomato purée for a few minutes, stirring to blend the flavours. Remove from the heat and stir in the shredded chicken, mixing well.

4 Spread about 30ml/2 tbsp of the chicken mixture on each pair of tortillas, roll them up into flutes and secure with a cocktail stick.

5 Heat a little oil in a frying pan large enough to hold the flutes comfortably. Cook more than one at a time if possible, but don't overcrowd the pan. Fry the flutes until light brown all over. Add more oil if needed.

6 Drain the cooked flutes on kitchen paper, and keep hot. When ready to serve, transfer to a platter and garnish with radishes and olives.

--- COOK'S TIP ---

If the flour tortillas are too hard to roll up easily, fry them for just a few seconds in hot oil, then quickly stuff and roll them.

Chilaquiles

INGREDIENTS

Serves 4

corn or peanut oil, for frying
6 leftover corn tortillas, cut or torn into
  1cm/½in strips
275g/10oz can tomatillos (Mexican
  green tomatoes)
1 onion, finely chopped
2–3 drained canned *jalapeño* chillies,
  rinsed, seeded and chopped
30ml/2 tbsp chopped fresh coriander
115g/4oz/1 cup grated Cheddar cheese
175ml/6fl oz/ ¾ cup chicken stock
salt and freshly ground black pepper

To garnish

chopped spring onion
stuffed green olives
chopped fresh coriander

1 Heat 45ml/3 tbsp of the oil in a
large frying pan. Fry the tortilla
strips, a few at a time, on both sides,
without browning. Add more oil if
needed. Drain on kitchen paper.

2 Tip the tomatillos and juice into a
food processor. Add the onion,
chillies and coriander; purée.

3 Season the tomatillo purée with
salt and pepper. Heat 15ml/1 tbsp
oil in the clean frying pan, add the
tomatillo mixture and cook gently for
2–3 minutes, stirring frequently.

4 Pour a layer of the sauce into the
bottom of a flameproof casserole
or shallow baking dish and top with a
layer of tortilla strips and a layer of
grated cheese. Continue until all the
ingredients have been used, reserving
some cheese for sprinkling on top.

5 Pour the chicken stock over the
dish and sprinkle with the reserved
cheese. If using a flameproof casserole,
cover and cook over a moderate heat
until all the liquid has been absorbed
and the dish is heated through. Or,
bake the chilaquiles, uncovered, in a
preheated oven at 180°C/350°F/Gas 4
for 30 minutes or until heated through.

6 Serve directly from the casserole
or dish, garnished with chopped
spring onion, olives and coriander.

Tamales de Picadillo

In ancient times these little parcels were cooked in the hot ashes of a camp fire.

INGREDIENTS

12 dried corn husks
50g/2oz/¼ cup lard
150g/5oz/1 cup *masa harina*
  (tortilla flour)
2.5ml/½ tsp salt
5ml/1 tsp baking powder
175ml/6fl oz/¾ cup chicken stock
½ quantity Picadillo

1 Soak the corn husks in warm water for about 2 hours until pliable.

2 In a bowl, cream the lard until it is very light and fluffy. Mix the *masa harina* with the salt and baking powder and beat it into the lard, bit by bit.

3 Warm the chicken stock. It should not be hot or it will melt the lard. Gradually beat enough of the stock into the flour mixture to make a mushy dough. To see if the dough is ready, carefully place a small piece on top of a bowl of water. If it floats, the dough is ready; if it sinks, continue to beat the dough until it is light enough to float.

4 Drain a corn husk and lay it flat on a board. Spread about 30ml/2 tbsp of the dough down the centre part of the husk, leaving plenty of room all round for folding. Spoon 30ml/2 tbsp of the Picadillo on to the centre of the dough. Roll up the husk from one long side, Swiss-roll fashion, so that the filling is completely enclosed, then fold the ends of the husks under. Make more tamales in the same way.

5 Prepare a steamer or use a metal colander and a deep saucepan into which the colander will fit with about 2.5cm/1in space all around.

6 Put the tamales in the steamer, folded ends under. Alternatively, place them in the colander and pour boiling water into the pan to within 2.5cm/1in of the bottom of the colander. Steam the tamales for about 1 hour, or until the dough comes away from the husk. Top up the water as required. Serve the tamales in the husk, leaving the diners to open them at the table to reveal the filling inside.

VARIATIONS

Any shredded cooked meat, moistened with salsa, can be used for the filling of these *tamales*. Alternatively, use strips of seeded *jalapeño* chilli and Cheddar cheese. If you have any leftover Mole Poblano de Guajolote, use 25ml/1½ tbsp to fill each tamale. *Tamales de Oaxaca* uses banana leaves softened in hot water and cut into 25cm/10in squares, instead of corn husks.

Red Enchiladas

INGREDIENTS

Serves 6

4 dried *ancho* chillies
450g/1lb tomatoes, peeled, seeded
  and chopped
1 onion, finely chopped
1 garlic clove, chopped
15ml/1 tbsp chopped fresh coriander
lard or corn oil for frying
250ml/8fl oz/1 cup soured cream
4 chorizo sausages, skinned
  and chopped
18 freshly prepared unbaked
  corn tortillas
50g/2oz/2½ cups freshly grated
  Parmesan cheese
salt and freshly ground black pepper

1 Roast the *ancho* chillies in a dry frying pan over moderate heat for 1–2 minutes, shaking the pan frequently. When cool, carefully slit the chillies, remove the stems and seeds, and tear the pods into pieces. Put in a bowl, add warm water to just cover, and soak for 20 minutes.

2 Tip the chillies, with a little of the soaking water, into a food processor. Add the tomatoes, onion, garlic and coriander; purée.

COOK'S TIP

The method of dipping the tortillas first in sauce, then quickly cooking them in lard or oil gives the best flavour. If you prefer, fry the plain tortillas very quickly, then dip them in the sauce, stuff and roll. There is not a great loss of flavour, and no spatter.

3 Heat 15ml/1 tbsp lard or oil in a saucepan. Add the purée and cook gently over a moderate heat, stirring, for 3–4 minutes. Season to taste with salt and pepper and then stir in the soured cream. Remove the pan from the heat and set it aside.

4 Heat a further 15ml/1 tbsp lard or oil in a small frying pan; sauté the chorizo for a few minutes until lightly browned. Moisten with a little of the sauce and set the pan aside.

5 Preheat the oven to 180°C/350°F/ Gas 4. Heat 30ml/2 tbsp lard or oil in a frying pan. Dip a tortilla in the sauce and add to the pan. Cook for a few seconds, shaking the pan gently, turn over and briefly fry the other side.

6 Slide the tortilla on to a plate, top with some of the sausage mixture, and roll up. Pack the prepared tortillas in a single layer in a baking dish. Pour the sauce over, sprinkle with Parmesan and bake for about 20 minutes.

Chimichangas

INGREDIENTS

Makes 14
½ quantity Picadillo
14 freshly prepared unbaked
    flour tortillas
oil, for frying

To garnish
whole radishes with leaves

COOK'S TIP

Chimichangas originally came from the
state of Sonora, and are made with the
large plate-sized tortillas that are a speciality
of the region. Any size that suits the cook
will do just as well.

1 Spoon about 60ml/4 tbsp Picadillo down the centre of each tortilla. Fold in the sides, then the top and bottom, envelope-fashion, or simply roll up and fasten with a cocktail stick.

2 Pour the corn oil into a frying pan to a depth of about 2.5cm/1in. Set the pan over a moderate heat. Fry the chimichangas, a few at a time, for about 1–2 minutes, or until golden.

3 Drain on kitchen paper and keep warm. Serve the chimichangas garnished with whole radishes.

Tacos

The taco has been called the Mexican sandwich; it is always eaten in the hand and makes a great speedy snack. All you need is a supply of tortillas or taco shells, and a selection of fillings.

INGREDIENTS

Makes as many as you like
freshly prepared corn tortillas or pre-
    prepared taco shells

For the fillings
Picadillo topped with Guacamole
chopped chorizo fried and mixed with
    chopped Cheddar cheese and chillies
Frijoles Refritos (Refried Beans) with
    sliced *jalapeño* chillies, Guacamole,
    and cubed cheese
leftover Mole Poblano de Guajolote
    with Guacamole
cooked shredded pork or chicken with
    salsa and shredded lettuce

1 To make tacos, all you need is a supply of fresh corn tortillas, and as many of the suggested fillings as you can muster. The idea is to use your imagination, and cooks often vie with one another to see who can produce the most interesting combination of flavours. Chillies and guacamole are always welcome, in the taco or served as an extra on the side.

2 To make traditional soft tacos, simply spoon the filling on to the tortilla, wrap the tortilla around the filling – and eat.

3 To make hard tacos, secure the rolled up and filled tortilla with a cocktail stick, then briefly shallow fry until crisp and golden.

4 Pre-prepared U-shaped taco shells are not Mexican, but make a speedy version of this snack. Hold one taco shell at a time in one hand, and fill with the fillings of your choice.

SOUPS

Soups are a must for the midday main meal, comida. There are two types, aguada *(liquid) and* seca *(dry). The first term is self-explanatory, but what exactly is a "dry soup"? It describes a separate course – traditionally a tortilla or rice dish – served after the more conventional soup and before the main course. Mexican cooks set great store by the quality of their home-made chicken and beef stocks. Either of these can be served as a soup in its own right with the addition of rice, or chick-peas (garbanzos).*

Vermicelli Soup

INGREDIENTS

Serves 4

30ml/2 tbsp olive or corn oil
50g/2oz/⅓ cup vermicelli
1 onion, roughly chopped
1 garlic clove, chopped
450g/1lb tomatoes, peeled, seeded and
    roughly chopped
1 litre/1¾ pints/4 cups chicken stock
1.5ml/¼ tsp sugar
15ml/1 tbsp finely chopped
    fresh coriander
salt and freshly ground black pepper
chopped fresh coriander, to garnish
25g/1oz/¼ cup freshly grated Parmesan
    cheese, to serve

COOK'S TIP

Vermicelli burns very easily, so move it
about continuously in the frying pan with a
wooden spoon and remove it from the heat
as soon as it is golden brown.

1 Heat the oil in a frying pan and
    sauté the vermicelli over a
moderate heat until golden brown.
Take care not to let the strands burn.
Remove the vermicelli with a slotted
spoon and drain on kitchen paper.

2 Purée the onion, garlic and
    tomatoes in a food processor until
smooth. Return the frying pan to the
heat. When the oil is hot, add the
purée. Cook, stirring constantly, for
about 5 minutes or until thick.

3 Transfer the purée to a saucepan.
    Add the vermicelli and pour in the
stock. Season with sugar, salt and
pepper. Stir in the coriander, bring to
the boil, then lower the heat, cover the
pan and simmer the soup until the
vermicelli is tender.

4 Serve in heated bowls, sprinkle
    with chopped fresh coriander and
offer the Parmesan separately.

Tomato Soup

INGREDIENTS

Serves 4

15ml/1 tbsp corn or peanut oil
1 onion, finely chopped
900g/2lb tomatoes, peeled, seeded
    and chopped
475ml/16fl oz/2 cups chicken stock
2 large fresh coriander sprigs
salt and freshly ground black pepper
coarsely ground black pepper, to serve

1 Heat the oil in a large saucepan
    and gently fry the finely chopped
onion, stirring frequently, for about
5 minutes, or until it is soft and
transparent but not brown.

2 Add the chopped tomatoes,
    chicken stock and coriander sprigs
to the pan. Bring to the boil, then
lower the heat, cover the pan and
simmer gently for about 15 minutes.

3 Remove and discard the coriander.
    Press the soup through a sieve and
return it to the clean pan. Season and
heat through. Serve sprinkled with
coarsely ground black pepper.

Corn Soup

This is a simple-to-make yet very flavoursome soup. It is sometimes made with soured cream and cream cheese. *Poblano* chillies may be added, but these are rather difficult to locate outside Mexico.

INGREDIENTS

Serves 4

30ml/2 tbsp corn oil
1 onion, finely chopped
1 red pepper, seeded and chopped
450g/1lb sweetcorn kernels, thawed
   if frozen
750ml/1¼ pints/3 cups chicken stock
250ml/8fl oz/1 cup single cream
salt and freshly ground black pepper
½ red pepper, seeded and cut in small
   dice, to garnish

1 Heat the oil in a frying pan and sauté the onion and red pepper for about 5 minutes, until soft. Add the sweetcorn and sauté for 2 minutes.

2 Carefully tip the contents of the pan into a food processor or blender. Process until smooth, scraping down the sides and adding a little of the stock, if necessary.

3 Put the mixture into a saucepan and stir in the stock. Season to taste with salt and pepper, bring to a simmer and cook for 5 minutes.

4 Gently stir in the cream. Serve the soup hot or chilled, sprinkled with the diced red pepper. If serving hot, reheat gently after adding the cream, but do not allow the soup to boil.

Courgette Soup

INGREDIENTS

Serves 4

30ml/2 tbsp butter
1 onion, finely chopped
450g/1lb young courgettes, trimmed
   and chopped
750ml/1¼ pints/3 cups chicken stock
120ml/4fl oz/½ cup single cream, plus
   extra to serve
salt and freshly ground black pepper

COOK'S TIP

Always use the smallest courgettes available. This is how they are preferred in Mexico, their country of origin.

---

1 Melt the butter in a saucepan and sauté the onion until it is soft. Add the courgettes and cook, stirring, for about 1–2 minutes.

2 Add the chicken stock. Bring to the boil over a moderate heat and simmer for about 5 minutes or until the courgettes are just tender.

3 Strain the stock into a clean saucepan, saving the vegetable solids in the sieve. Purée the solids in a food processor and add to the pan. Season to taste with salt and pepper.

4 Stir the cream into the soup and heat through very gently without allowing it to boil. Serve hot with a little extra cream swirled in.

Sopa Seca de Tortilla con Crema

Dry soup is a separate course that follows liquid soup (*sopa aguada*) in the main meal or *comida*.

INGREDIENTS

Serves 6

120ml/4fl oz/½ cup corn oil
1 onion, finely chopped
2 garlic cloves, chopped
450g/1lb tomatoes, peeled, seeded and
    finely chopped
2.5ml/½ tsp dried oregano
1.5ml/¼ tsp sugar
16 small, day-old corn tortillas, cut into
    1cm/½ in strips
250ml/8fl oz/1 cup double cream
115g/4oz/1 cup freshly grated
    Parmesan cheese
salt and freshly ground black pepper

1 Heat 30ml/2 tbsp of oil in a frying pan. Sauté the onion and garlic until soft and stir in the tomatoes.

COOK'S TIP

Be sure to use corn tortillas for this recipe. If only large ones are available, use eight.

2 Cook the tomatoes until thick, then stir in the oregano and sugar. Season and put in a bowl. Set aside.

3 Heat the remaining oil in the clean pan and fry the tortillas without browning. Drain on kitchen paper.

4 Pour a layer of tomato sauce into a greased flameproof casserole. Add a layer of tortilla strips, a thin layer of cream, another layer of sauce, and a layer of grated cheese. Continue until all the ingredients have been used, ending with a layer of cheese. Cover the casserole and heat through gently on top of the stove. (Or, heat through in a preheated 180°C/350°F/Gas 4 oven for about 20 minutes.)

Mexican-style Rice

INGREDIENTS

Serves 6

350g/12oz/1¾ cups long grain
  white rice
1 onion, chopped
2 garlic cloves, chopped
450g/1lb tomatoes, peeled, seeded and
  coarsely chopped
60ml/4 tbsp corn or peanut oil
900ml/1½ pints/3¾ cups chicken stock
4 – 6 small red chillies
175g/6oz/1 cup cooked green peas
salt and freshly ground black pepper
fresh coriander sprigs, to garnish

1 Soak the rice in a bowl of hot water for 15 minutes. Drain, rinse well under cold running water, drain again and set aside.

2 Combine the onion, garlic and tomatoes in a food processor and process to a purée.

3 Heat the oil in a large frying pan. Add the drained rice and sauté until it is golden brown. Using a slotted spoon, transfer the rice to a saucepan.

4 Reheat the oil remaining in the pan and cook the tomato purée for 2–3 minutes. Tip it into the saucepan and pour in the stock. Season to taste. Bring to the boil, reduce the heat to the lowest possible setting, cover the pan and cook for 15–20 minutes until almost all the liquid has been absorbed. Slice the red chillies from tip to stem end into four or five sections. Place in a bowl of iced water until they curl back to form flowers, then drain.

5 Stir the peas into the rice mixture and cook, without a lid, until all the liquid has been absorbed and the rice is tender. Stir the mixture from time to time.

6 Transfer the rice to a serving dish and garnish with the drained chilli flowers and sprigs of coriander. Warn the diners that these elaborate chilli "flowers" are hot and should be approached with caution.

Tlalpeño-style Soup

For a hearty version of this
simple soup, add some cooked
chick-peas or rice.

INGREDIENTS

Serves 6

1.5 litres/2½ pints/6 cups chicken stock
2 cooked chicken breast fillets, skinned
    and cut into large strips
1 drained canned *chipotle* chilli or
    jalapeño chilli, rinsed
1 avocado

―――――― COOK'S TIP ――――――

When using canned chillies, it is important
to rinse them very thoroughly before
adding them to the pan so as to remove the
flavour of any pickling liquid.

1 Heat the stock in a large saucepan
and add the chicken and chilli.
Simmer over a very gentle heat for
5 minutes to heat the chicken and
release the flavour from the chilli.

2 Cut the avocado in half, remove
the stone and peel off the skin.
Slice the avocado flesh neatly.

3 Remove the chilli from the stock,
using a slotted spoon, and then
discard it. Pour the soup into heated
serving bowls, distributing the chicken
evenly among them.

4 Carefully add a few avocado slices
to each bowl and serve.

Avocado Soup

INGREDIENTS

Serves 4

2 large ripe avocados
1 litre/1¾ pints/4 cups chicken stock
250ml/8fl oz/1 cup single cream
salt and freshly ground white pepper
15ml/1 tbsp finely chopped coriander,
    to garnish (optional)

―――――― COOK'S TIP ――――――

The easiest way to mash the avocados is to
hold each seeded half in turn in the palm of
one hand and mash the flesh in the shell
with a fork, before scooping it into the
bowl. This avoids the avocado slithering
about when it is being mashed.

1 Cut the avocados in half, remove
the stones and mash the flesh (see
Cook's Tip). Put the flesh into a sieve
and with a wooden spoon, press it
through into a warm soup bowl.

2 Heat the chicken stock with the
cream in a saucepan. When the
mixture is hot, but not boiling, whisk
it into the puréed avocado.

3 Season to taste with salt and pepper.
Serve immediately, sprinkled with
the coriander, if used. The soup may be
served chilled, if liked.

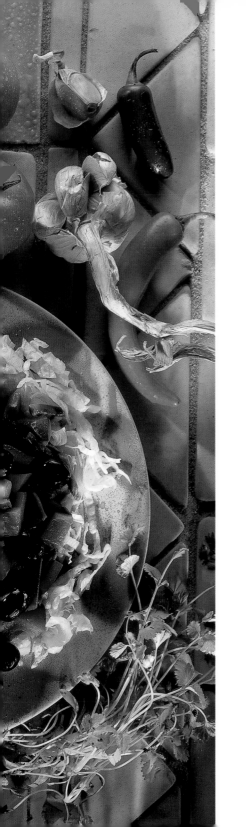

VEGETABLES
AND
SALADS

Mexico is blessed with a bounty of vegetables. The New World vegetables first cultivated by the Aztec and Maya-Toltec civilisations thousands of years ago include corn, all the peppers (sweet, pungent and hot), tomatoes, common beans like red and black kidney beans, pinto beans, pumpkins, courgettes, chayote (chocho), avocados, potatoes, sweet potatoes, and lima beans from the Inca Empire, now modern Peru and Bolivia. The Spanish Conquistadores brought in European vegetables like cabbage, chick-peas, cucumbers, regional types of onion and garlic, cauliflowers, turnips, green peas and aubergines. As a result of the marriage of foods and cooking methods, many new dishes were created, especially salads.

Frijoles

INGREDIENTS

Serves 6–8

350g/12oz/1¼–1½ cups dried red
kidney, pinto or black haricot beans,
picked over and rinsed
2 onions, finely chopped
2 garlic cloves, chopped
1 bay leaf
1 or more *serrano* chillies (small fresh
green chillies)
30ml/2 tbsp corn oil
2 tomatoes, peeled, seeded and
chopped
salt
sprigs of fresh bay leaves, to garnish

— COOK'S TIP —

In Yucatan black haricot beans are cooked
with the Mexican herb *epazote*.

---

1 Put the beans into a pan and add
cold water to cover by 2.5cm/1in.

2 Add half the onion, half the garlic,
the bay leaf and the chilli(es). Bring
to the boil and boil vigorously for
about 10 minutes. Put the beans and
liquid into an earthenware pot or large
saucepan, cover and cook over a low
heat for 30 minutes. Add boiling water
if the mixture starts to become dry.

3 When the beans begin to wrinkle,
add 15ml/1 tbsp of the corn oil
and cook for a further 30 minutes or
until the beans are tender. Add salt to
taste and cook for 30 minutes more,
but do not add any more water.

4 Remove the beans from the heat.
Heat the remaining oil in a small
frying pan and sauté the remaining
onion and garlic until the onion is soft
Add the tomatoes and cook for a few
minutes more.

5 Spoon 45ml/3 tbsp of the beans
out of the pot or pan and add
them to the tomato mixture. Mash to
paste. Stir this into the beans to thicken
the liquid. Cook for just long enough
to heat through, if necessary. Serve the
beans in small bowls and garnish with
sprigs of fresh bay leaves.

Peppers Stuffed with Beans

Stuffed peppers are a popular Mexican dish. A special version – *Chiles en Nogada* – is served every year on August 28 to celebrate Independence Day. The green peppers are served with a sauce of fresh walnuts and a garnish of pomegranate seeds to represent the colours of the Mexican flag.

INGREDIENTS

Serves 6
6 large green peppers
1 quantity Frijoles Refritos (Refried Beans)
2 eggs, separated
2.5ml/½ tsp salt
corn oil, for frying
plain flour, for dusting
120ml/4fl oz/½ cup whipping cream
115g/4oz/1 cup grated Cheddar cheese
fresh coriander sprigs, to garnish

1 Roast the peppers over a gas flame or under a medium grill, turning occasionally, until the skins have blackened and blistered. Transfer the peppers to a plastic bag, secure the top and leave for 15 minutes.

2 Preheat the oven to 180°C/350°F/ Gas 4. Remove the peppers from the bag. Hold each pepper in turn under cold running water and gently rub off the skins. Slit the peppers down one side and remove the seeds and ribs, taking care not to break the pepper shells. Stuff with the Refried Beans.

3 Beat the egg whites in a large bowl until they stand in firm peaks. In another bowl, beat the yolks lightly together with the salt. Fold the yolks gently into the whites.

4 Pour the corn oil into a large frying pan to a depth of about 2.5cm/1in and heat. Spread out the flour in a shallow bowl or dish.

5 Dip the filled peppers in the flour and then in the egg mixture. Fry in batches in the hot oil until golden brown all over. Arrange the peppers in an ovenproof dish. Pour over the cream and sprinkle with the cheese. Bake in the oven for 30 minutes or until the topping is golden brown and the peppers are heated through. Serve at once, garnished with fresh coriander.

Chopped Courgettes

Calabacitas is an extremely easy recipe to make. If the cooking time seems unduly long, this is because the acid present in the tomatoes slows down the cooking of the courgettes. Use young tender courgettes.

INGREDIENTS

Serves 4
30ml/2 tbsp corn oil
450g/1lb young courgettes, sliced
1 onion, finely chopped
2 garlic cloves, chopped
450g/1lb tomatoes, peeled, seeded and chopped
2 drained canned *jalapeño* chillies, rinsed, seeded and chopped
15ml/1 tbsp chopped fresh coriander
salt
fresh coriander, to garnish

1 Heat the oil in a flameproof casserole and add all the remaining ingredients, except the salt.

2 Bring to simmering point, cover and cook over a low heat for about 30 minutes until the courgettes are tender, checking from time to time that the dish is not drying out. If it is, add a little tomato juice, stock or water.

3 Season with salt and serve the Mexican way as a separate course. Alternatively, serve accompanied by any plainly cooked meat or poultry. Garnish with fresh coriander.

Refried Beans (Frijoles Refritos)

There is much disagreement about the translation of the term *refrito*. It means, literally, twice fried. Some cooks say this implies that the beans must be really well fried, others that it means twice cooked. However named, *Frijoles Refritos* are delicious.

INGREDIENTS

Serves 6–8
90–120ml/6–8 tbsp lard or corn oil
1 onion, finely chopped
1 quantity Frijoles (cooked beans)

To garnish
freshly grated Parmesan cheese or crumbled cottage cheese
crisp fried corn tortillas, cut into quarters

1 Heat 30ml/2 tbsp of the lard in a large heavy-based frying pan and sauté the onion until it is soft. Add about 225ml/8fl oz/1 cup of the Frijoles (cooked beans).

— COOK'S TIP —

Lard is the traditional (and best tasting) fat for the beans but many people prefer to use corn oil. Avoid using olive oil, which is too strongly flavoured and distinctive.

2 Mash the beans with the back of a wooden spoon or potato masher, adding more beans and melted lard or oil until all the ingredients are used up and the beans have formed a heavy paste. Use extra lard or oil if necessary.

3 Tip out on to a warmed platter, piling the mixture up in a roll. Garnish with the cheese. Spike with the tortilla triangles, placing them at intervals along the length of the roll. Serve as a side dish.

Mushrooms with Chipotle Chillies

Ingredients

Serves 6

450g/1lb/4 cups button mushrooms
60ml/4 tbsp olive oil
1 onion, finely chopped
2 garlic cloves, chopped
2 drained canned *chipotle* chillies,
   rinsed and sliced
salt
chopped fresh coriander, to garnish

Cook's Tip

Never wash mushrooms as they quickly absorb water. Wipe them with kitchen paper or a clean, damp cloth.

1 Wipe the mushrooms gently and carefully with kitchen paper. Heat the olive oil in a large frying pan and add the mushrooms, finely chopped onion, chopped garlic, and sliced chillies. Stir to coat in oil.

2 Fry the mixture over a moderate heat for 6–8 minutes, stirring from time to time, until the onions and mushrooms are tender. Season to taste with salt and serve on small individual plates, sprinkled with a little chopped fresh coriander.

Prawn Salad

Salads in Mexico are usually served with the main course instead of green vegetables. Salads containing meat or seafood are served as a separate course, as they are very satisfying.

Ingredients

Serves 4

1 iceberg lettuce or 2 Little Gem
   lettuces, separated into leaves, or
   assorted lettuce leaves
60ml/4 tbsp mayonnaise
60ml/4 tbsp soured cream
350g/12oz cooked prawns, thawed if
   frozen, chopped
75g/3oz/½ cup cooked green
   beans, chopped
75g/3oz/½ cup cooked carrots,
   chopped
½ cucumber, about 115g/4oz chopped
2 hard-boiled eggs, coarsely chopped
1 drained pickled *jalapeño* chilli, seeded
   and chopped
salt

1 Line a large salad bowl or platter with the lettuce leaves. Mix the mayonnaise and soured cream together in a small bowl and put aside.

2 Combine the prawns, beans, carrot, cucumber, eggs and chilli in a separate bowl. Season with salt.

3 Add the mayonnaise and soured cream mixture to the prawns, folding it in very gently so that all the ingredients are well mixed and coated with the dressing. Pile the mixture into the lined salad bowl or arrange attractively on the platter and serve.

Green Lima Beans in Sauce

A tasty dish of lima beans with a tomato and chilli sauce.

INGREDIENTS

Serves 4

450g/1lb green lima or broad beans, thawed if frozen
30ml/2 tbsp olive oil
1 onion, finely chopped
2 garlic cloves, chopped
350g/12oz tomatoes, peeled, seeded and chopped
1 or 2 drained canned *jalapeño* chillies, seeded and chopped
salt
chopped fresh coriander sprigs, to garnish

1 Cook the beans in a saucepan of boiling water for 15–20 minutes until tender. Drain and keep hot, to one side, in the covered saucepan.

2 Heat the olive oil in a frying pan and sauté the onion and garlic until the onion is soft but not brown. Add the tomatoes and cook until the mixture is thick and flavoursome.

3 Add the *jalapeños* and cook for 1–2 minutes. Season with salt.

4 Pour the mixture over the reserved beans and check that they are hot. If not, return everything to the frying pan and cook over low heat for just long enough to heat through. Put into a warm serving dish, garnish with the coriander and serve.

Green Bean and Sweet Red Pepper Salad

INGREDIENTS

Serves 4

350g/12oz cooked green beans,
  quartered
2 red peppers, seeded and chopped
2 spring onions (white and green parts),
  chopped
1 or more drained pickled *serrano*
  chillies, well rinsed and then seeded
  and chopped
1 iceberg lettuce, coarsely shredded, or
  mixed salad leaves
olives, to garnish

For the dressing

45ml/3 tbsp red wine vinegar
135ml/9 tbsp olive oil
salt and freshly ground black pepper

1 Combine the cooked green beans,
  chopped peppers, chopped spring
onions and chillies in a salad bowl.

2 Make the salad dressing. Pour the
  red wine vinegar into a bowl or
jug. Add salt and freshly ground black
pepper to taste, then gradually whisk in
the olive oil until well combined.

3 Pour the salad dressing over the
  prepared vegetables and toss lightly
together to mix and coat thoroughly.

4 Line a large platter with the
  shredded lettuce leaves and arrange
the salad attractively on top. Garnish
with the olives and serve.

Avocado and Tomato Salad

INGREDIENTS

Serves 4

2 ripe avocados
2 large beefsteak tomatoes, about
   225g/8oz each, peeled and seeded
1 iceberg lettuce, coarsely shredded, or
   mixed salad leaves
30ml/2 tbsp chopped fresh coriander
salt and freshly ground black pepper

For the dressing

90ml/6 tbsp olive or corn oil
30ml/2 tbsp fresh lemon juice

1 Cut the avocados in half, remove the stones and peel off the skin. Then cut the avocados and tomatoes into equal numbers of lengthways slices of approximately the same size.

2 Arrange a bed of shredded lettuce on a large platter and place the tomato slices on top. Arrange the avocado slices over the tomato and sprinkle with the coriander. Season to taste with salt and pepper.

3 Whisk the olive or corn oil and lemon juice together in a jug until well combined.

4 Pour a little dressing over the salad and serve the rest separately.

> ——— COOK'S TIP ———
>
> To ripen avocados, put them in a brown paper bag and store in a dark place for several days, checking from time to time. They are ready when they yield to a gentle pressure at the stem end.

Chayote Salad

Chayote goes by several different names – chocho, christophine or vegetable pear being the most familiar. Native to Mexico, they are now widely cultivated in the Caribbean, South East Asia and parts of Africa.

INGREDIENTS

Serves 4

2 chayotes, peeled and halved
1 large beefsteak tomato, about
   225g/8oz, peeled and cut into
   6 wedges
1 small onion, finely chopped

For the dressing

2.5ml/½ tsp Dijon mustard
30ml/2 tbsp mild white vinegar
90ml/6 tbsp olive or corn oil
salt and freshly ground black pepper
strips of seeded pickled *jalapeño* chillies,
   to garnish

1 Leaving the seeds in place, cook the chayotes in a large saucepan of boiling salted water for about 20 minutes or until tender. Drain and leave to cool. Remove the seeds and set them aside (see Cook's Tip). Cut the flesh into chunks about the same size as the tomato wedges.

2 Make the dressing directly in a salad bowl. Combine the Dijon mustard and the vinegar with salt and pepper to taste. Gradually whisk in the oil until well combined.

3 Put the chayote chunks, tomato wedges and finely chopped onion into a bowl. Add the dressing and toss gently together until well coated.

4 Put in a serving dish, garnish with the chilli strips and serve.

> ——— COOK'S TIP ———
>
> The seed of the chayote is edible and makes an admirable cook's perk.

FISH AND SHELLFISH

Mexico has an extensive coastline and an abundance of fish and shellfish, many of which are available here, often in Caribbean markets. The catch includes red snapper, mackerel, sea bass, striped bass, and prawns. Red snapper is used for the nation's most famous dish, Huachinango a la Veracruzana *(Red Snapper, Veracruz-style). Another world-renowned dish is Seviche, which may be a Mexican invention, or could have originated in Polynesia. This delectable starter consists of fish "cooked" in lime or lemon juice. Thanks to the influence of Spain and Portugal, there are also numerous dishes made with that perennial favourite, dried salt cod. Most of the following fish dishes can be made using fillets of any firm-fleshed non-oily fish.*

Striped Bass in Sauce

This is a typical Mayan dish.

INGREDIENTS

Serves 6

1.5kg/3–3½lb striped bass or any non-
  oily white fish, cut into 6 steaks
120ml/4fl oz/½ cup corn oil
1 large onion, thinly sliced
2 garlic cloves, chopped
350g/12oz tomatoes, sliced
2 drained canned *jalapeño* chillies,
  rinsed and sliced

For the marinade

4 garlic cloves, crushed
5ml/1 tsp black peppercorns
5ml/1 tsp dried oregano
2.5ml/½tsp ground cumin
5ml/1 tsp ground *achiote* (annatto)
2.5ml/½tsp ground cinnamon
120ml/4fl oz/½ cup mild white vinegar
salt
flat leaf parsley, to garnish

1 Arrange the fish steaks in a single
layer in a shallow dish. Make the
marinade. Using a pestle, grind the
garlic and black peppercorns in a
mortar. Add the dried oregano, cumin,
achiote (annatto) and cinnamon and mix
to a paste with the vinegar. Add salt to
taste and spread the marinade on both
sides of each of the fish steaks. Cover
and leave in a cool place for 1 hour.

2 Select a flameproof dish large
enough to hold the fish in a single
layer and pour in enough of the oil to
coat the bottom. Arrange the fish in
the dish with any remaining marinade.

3 Top the fish with the onion, garlic,
tomatoes and chillies and pour the
rest of the oil over the top.

4 Cover the dish and cook over a
low heat on top of the stove for
15–20 minutes, or until the fish is no
longer translucent. Serve at once
garnished with flat leaf parsley.

Salt Cod in Mild Chilli Sauce

INGREDIENTS

Serves 6
900g/2lb dried salt cod
1 onion, chopped
2 garlic cloves, chopped

For the sauce
6 dried *ancho* chillies
1 onion, chopped
2.5ml/½ tsp dried oregano
2.5ml/½ tsp ground coriander
1 *serrano* chilli, seeded and chopped
45ml/3 tbsp corn oil
750ml/1¼ pints/3 cups fish or
   chicken stock
salt

For the garnish
1 fresh green chilli, sliced

> ──── COOK'S TIP ────
>
> Dried salt cod is a great favourite in Spain
> and Portugal and throughout Latin
> America. Look for it in Spanish and
> Portuguese markets.

1 Soak the cod in cold water for several hours, depending on how hard and salty it is. Change the water once or twice during soaking.

2 Drain the fish and transfer it to a saucepan. Pour in water to cover. Bring to a gentle simmer and cook for about 15 minutes until the fish is tender. Drain, reserving the stock. Remove any skin or bones from the fish and cut it into 4cm/1½in pieces.

3 Make the sauce. Remove the stems and shake out the seeds from the *ancho* chillies. Tear the pods into pieces, put in a bowl of warm water and soak until they are soft.

4 Drain the soaked chillies and put them into a food processor with the onion, oregano, coriander and *serrano* chilli. Process to a purée.

5 Heat the oil in a frying pan and cook the purée, stirring, for about 5 minutes. Stir in the fish or chicken stock and simmer for 3–4 minutes.

6 Add the prepared cod and simmer for a few minutes longer to heat the fish through and blend the flavours. Serve garnished with the sliced chilli.

Crab with Green Rice

INGREDIENTS

Serves 4

225g/8oz/1 cup long grain rice
60ml/4 tbsp olive oil
2 x 275g/10oz cans tomatillos
    (Mexican green tomatoes)
1 onion, chopped
2 garlic cloves, chopped
30ml/2 tbsp chopped fresh coriander
about 350ml/12fl oz/1½ cups
    chicken stock
450g/1lb crab meat, thawed if frozen,
    broken into chunks
salt
chopped fresh coriander, to garnish
lettuce leaves, to serve

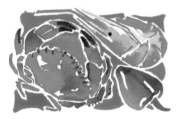

1 Soak the rice in enough hot water to cover for 15 minutes, then drain thoroughly. Heat the oil in a frying pan and sauté the rice over a moderate heat, stirring until the rice is golden and the oil has been absorbed.

2 Drain the tomatillos, reserving the juice, and put them into a food processor. Add the onion, garlic and coriander, and process to a purée. Pour into a measuring jug and add the tomatillo juice. Pour in enough stock to make the quantity up to 475ml/16fl oz/2 cups. Season to taste.

3 Place the rice, tomato mixture and crab meat in a shallow pan. Cover and cook over a very low heat for about 30 minutes or until the liquid has been absorbed and the rice is tender. Serve on lettuce leaves, garnished with chopped fresh coriander.

COOK'S TIP

Mexican cooks always soak rice in water before cooking it. This seems to pay off, as their rice is always delicious, with every grain separate.

Prawns with Pumpkin Seed Sauce

INGREDIENTS

Serves 4

175g/6oz/1 generous cup *pepitas*
    (Mexican pumpkin seeds)
450g/1lb raw prawns, thawed if frozen,
    peeled and deveined
1 onion, chopped
1 garlic clove, chopped
30ml/2 tbsp chopped fresh coriander
225g/8oz tomatoes, peeled
    and chopped
1 drained canned *jalapeño* chilli, rinsed,
    seeded and chopped
1 red pepper, seeded and chopped
30ml/2 tbsp corn oil
salt
whole cooked prawns, lemon slices and
    fresh coriander sprigs, to garnish
rice, to serve

1 Grind the pumpkin seeds finely and shake through a sieve into a bowl and set to one side.

2 Cook the prawns in boiling salted water. As soon as they turn pink, remove with a slotted spoon and set them aside. Reserve the cooking water.

3 Purée the onion, garlic, coriander, tomatoes, chilli, red pepper and pumpkin seeds in a food processor. Heat the oil in a pan, stir and cook the mixture for 5 minutes. Season. Add prawn water to thin the mixture to a sauce consistency. Heat gently, add the prawns. Garnish and serve with rice.

Seviche

This makes an excellent starter. With the addition of sliced avocado, it could make a light summer lunch for four.

INGREDIENTS

Serves 6

450g/1lb mackerel fillets, cut into 1cm/½in pieces
350ml/12fl oz/1½ cups freshly squeezed lime or lemon juice
225g/8oz tomatoes, chopped
1 small onion, very finely chopped
2 drained canned *jalapeño* chillies or 4 *serrano* chillies, rinsed and chopped
60ml/4 tbsp olive oil
2.5ml/½tsp dried oregano
30ml/2 tbsp chopped fresh coriander
salt and freshly ground black pepper
lemon wedges and fresh coriander, to garnish
stuffed green olives, to serve

1 Put the fish into a glass dish and pour over the lime or lemon juice, making sure that the fish is completely covered. Cover and chill for 6 hours, turning once, by which time the fish will be opaque, "cooked" by the juice.

--- COOK'S TIP ---

For a more delicately flavoured Seviche, use a white fish such as sole.

2 When the fish is opaque, lift it out of the juice and set it aside.

3 Combine the tomatoes, onion, chillies, olive oil, oregano and coriander in a bowl. Add salt and pepper to taste and then pour in the reserved juice from the mackerel. Mix well and pour over the fish.

4 Cover the dish and return the seviche to the fridge for about an hour to allow the flavours to blend. Seviche should not be served too cold. Allow it to stand at room temperature for 15 minutes before serving. Garnish with lemon wedges and coriander sprigs, and serve with stuffed olives sprinkled with chopped coriander.

Red Snapper with Coriander

As it is caught in the Gulf of Mexico, red snapper is used in this dish, but you can use any fillets of firm white fish instead.

INGREDIENTS

Serves 4

900g/2lb red snapper fillets or other white fish fillets
90ml/6 tbsp lime or lemon juice
60ml/4 tbsp olive oil
1 onion, finely chopped
50g/2oz/1 cup fresh coriander, finely chopped
2 drained canned *jalapeño* chillies, rinsed, seeded and sliced
salt and freshly ground black pepper
tomato rice, to serve

1 Place the fish in a shallow dish. Season with salt and pepper and drizzle the lime or lemon juice over. Cover and set aside for 15 minutes.

2 Preheat the oven to 180°C/350°F/ Gas 4. Heat all but 15ml/1 tbsp of the oil in a frying pan and sauté the onion until it is soft.

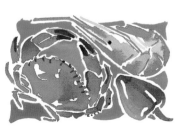

3 Use the reserved oil to thinly coat the bottom of an ovenproof dish which is just large enough to hold the fish fillets in a single layer. Arrange the fish in the dish and pour over any of the remaining marinating liquid. Top with the sautéed onion and the oil from the pan.

4 Sprinkle over the coriander and chillies. Bake for 20–25 minutes, or until the fish is no longer translucent. Serve with tomato rice.

— COOK'S TIP —

This may seem like a lot of coriander but it cooks down with the chillies, onion and pan juices to make a delicious sauce.

Prawns in Sauce

This colourful dish is called *Camarones en Salsa* in Mexico – serve it with rice, if you like.

INGREDIENTS

Serves 4

60ml/4 tbsp olive or corn oil
1 red pepper, seeded and chopped
2 large spring onions (white and green parts), chopped
2 garlic cloves, chopped
450g/1lb tomatoes, peeled, seeded and chopped
60ml/4 tbsp chopped fresh coriander
a little chicken stock
450g/1lb raw or cooked prawns, thawed if frozen, peeled and deveined
salt and freshly ground black pepper
fresh coriander, to garnish

1 Heat the oil in a flameproof casserole and sauté the pepper, spring onions and garlic until the pepper is soft. Add the tomatoes and simmer for about 10 minutes or until the mixture is thick and flavoursome.

2 Add the coriander and salt and pepper to taste. If the sauce is very thick, thin with chicken stock.

3 Add the prawns and cook for 2–3 minutes, depending on the size, until they turn pink. Be very careful not to overcook the prawns as they will toughen very quickly. Serve at once, with rice if liked, and garnish with fresh coriander.

Fish in Parsley Sauce

INGREDIENTS

Serves 6

275g/10oz can tomatillos (Mexican green tomatoes)
1 onion, finely chopped
2 garlic cloves, chopped
50g/2oz/1 cup flat leaf parsley, finely chopped
60ml/4 tbsp olive oil
6 firm-fleshed white fish fillets
salt and freshly ground black pepper

To garnish

drained canned *serrano* chillies, seeded, rinsed and shredded
sliced black olives

COOK'S TIP

Flat leaf or continental parsley has much more flavour than curly parsley. Keep the curly variety for use as a decoration and use the flat leaf parsley in cooking.

1 Drain the tomatillos, reserving the liquid. Mash them in a bowl with the onion, garlic and parsley. Season with salt and pepper and set aside.

2 Heat the oil in a large frying pan and sauté the fish fillets until they are golden on both sides. Using a fish slice, transfer the fillets to a warmed serving dish, cover and keep hot.

3 Heat the oil remaining in the pan and add the tomatillo mixture. Cook over a moderate heat, stirring from time to time, until the sauce is well blended and has the consistency of single cream. If it is too thick, add a little of the reserved tomatillo juice. Season to taste with salt and pepper.

4 Pour the sauce over the fish fillets, garnish with the *serrano* chillies and black olives and serve.

Pickled Fish (Pescado en Escabeche)

INGREDIENTS

Serves 4

900g/2lb white fish fillets
60ml/4 tbsp freshly squeezed lime or
lemon juice
300ml/½ pint/1¼ cups olive or corn oil
2 whole cloves
6 peppercorns
2 garlic cloves
2.5ml/½ tsp ground cumin
2.5ml/½ tsp dried oregano
2 bay leaves
1 drained canned *jalapeño* chilli, seeded,
and cut into strips
1 onion, thinly sliced
250ml/8fl oz/1 cup white wine vinegar
250ml/8fl oz/1 cup olive or corn oil
salt

For the garnish

lettuce leaves
green olives

1 Cut the fish fillets into eight pieces and arrange them in a single layer in a shallow dish. Drizzle with the lime or lemon juice. Cover and marinate for 15 minutes, turning the fillets once.

2 Lift out the fillets with a fish slice, pat them dry with kitchen paper and season with salt. Heat 60ml/4 tbsp of the oil in a frying pan and sauté the fish until lightly golden brown. Transfer to a platter and set aside.

3 Combine the cloves, peppercorns, garlic, cumin, oregano, bay leaves, chilli and vinegar in a pan. Bring to the boil, then simmer for 3–4 minutes.

4 Add the remaining oil, and bring to a simmer. Pour over the fish. Cool, cover and chill for 24 hours. To serve, lift out the fillets with a fish slice and arrange on a serving dish. Garnish with lettuce and olives.

--- COOK'S TIP ---

To make the dish special, add an elaborate garnish of radishes, capers and chilli strips.

Red Snapper, Veracruz-style

This is Mexico's best-known fish dish. In Veracruz red snapper is always used but fillets of any firm-fleshed white fish can be substituted successfully.

INGREDIENTS

Serves 4

4 large red snapper fillets
30ml/2 tbsp freshly squeezed lime or
  lemon juice
120ml/4fl oz/½ cup olive oil
1 onion, finely chopped
2 garlic cloves, chopped
675g/1½lb tomatoes, peeled
  and chopped
1 bay leaf, plus a few sprigs to garnish
1.5ml/¼ tsp dried oregano
30ml/2 tbsp large capers, plus extra
  to serve (optional)
16 stoned green olives, halved
2 drained canned *jalapeño* chillies,
  seeded and cut into strips
butter, for frying
3 slices firm white bread, cut
  into triangles
salt and freshly ground black pepper

1 Arrange the fish fillets in a single layer in a shallow dish. Season with salt and pepper, drizzle with the lime or lemon juice and set aside.

2 Heat the oil in a large frying pan and sauté the onion and garlic until the onion is soft. Add the tomatoes and cook for about 10 minutes until the mixture is thick and flavoursome. Stir the mixture from time to time.

3 Stir in the bay leaf, oregano, capers, olives and chillies. Add the fish and cook over a very low heat for about 10 minutes or until tender.

─── COOK'S TIP ───

This dish can also be made with a whole fish, weighing about 1.5kg/3–3½lb. Bake together with the sauce, in a preheated oven at 160°C/325°F/Gas 3. Allow 10 minutes cooking time for every 2.5cm/1in thickness of the fish.

4 While the fish is cooking, heat the butter in a small frying pan and sauté the bread triangles until they are golden brown on both sides.

5 Transfer the fish to a heated platter, pour over the sauce and surround with the fried bread triangles. Garnish with bay leaves and serve with extra capers, if you like.

MEATS
AND
POULTRY

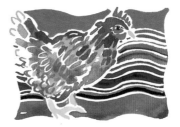

Wild boar roamed Mexico before the Conquest and there were some managed deer and animals related to the rabbit. The native inhabitants had domesticated the turkey, and also enjoyed dove, quail and pheasant (the curassow), but it took the Spanish Conquistadores to introduce the domestic hen. The Spaniards also brought cattle, sheep, goats and pigs. Apart from the great national festive dish, Mole Poblano de Guajolote made with turkey, other meat and poultry dishes were colonial, uniting foods and cooking methods from both the Old and New Worlds.

Pheasant in Green Pipian Sauce

INGREDIENTS

Serves 4

2 oven-ready pheasants
30ml/2 tbsp corn oil
175g/6oz/1 generous cup *pepitas*
  (Mexican pumpkin seeds)
15ml/1 tbsp *achiote* (annatto) seeds
1 onion, finely chopped
2 garlic cloves, chopped
275g/10oz can tomatillos (Mexican
  green tomatoes)
475ml/16fl oz/2 cups chicken stock
salt and freshly ground black pepper
fresh coriander, to garnish

COOK'S TIP

Achiote is a typical ingredient in Yucatán. It
adds a subtle flavour and an orange-red
colour. There is no substitute. Look for it
in Caribbean and tropical markets.

1 Preheat the oven to 180°C/350°F/
Gas 4. Using a large sharp knife or
poultry shears, cut the pheasants in half
lengthways and season well with salt
and pepper. Heat the oil in a large
frying pan and sauté the pieces until
lightly brown on all sides. Lift out,
drain and arrange, skin-side up, in a
roasting tin large enough to hold them
comfortably in one layer. Set aside.

2 Grind the *pepitas* finely in a nut
grinder or a food processor. Shake
through a sieve into a bowl. Grind the
achiote seeds and add them to the bowl
and set to one side.

3 Put the onion, garlic, tomatillos
and their juice into a food
processor and purée. Put in a saucepan.

4 Add the *pepita* mixture, stir in the
stock and simmer over a very low
heat for 10 minutes. Do not let the
mixture boil as it will separate. Cool.

5 Pour over the pheasant halves.
Bake for 40 minutes, basting from
time to time with the sauce, or until
tender. Garnish with coriander.

Chicken in Green Almond Sauce

INGREDIENTS

Serves 6

1.5kg/3 – 3½lb chicken, cut into
  serving pieces
475ml/16fl oz/2 cups chicken stock
1 onion, chopped
1 garlic clove, chopped
115g/4oz/2 cups fresh coriander,
  coarsely chopped
1 green pepper, seeded and chopped
1 *jalapeño* chilli, seeded and chopped
275g/10oz can tomatillos (Mexican
  green tomatoes)
115g/4oz/1 cup ground almonds
30ml/2 tbsp corn oil
salt
fresh coriander, to garnish
rice, to serve

1 Put the chicken pieces into a
flameproof casserole or shallow
pan. Pour in the stock, bring to a
simmer, cover and cook for about 45
minutes, until tender. Drain the stock
into a measuring jug and set aside.

2 Put the onion, garlic, coriander,
green pepper, chilli, tomatillos
with their juice and the almonds in a
food processor. Purée fairly coarsely.

3 Heat the oil in a frying pan, add
the almond mixture and cook over
a low heat, stirring with a wooden
spoon, for 3 – 4 minutes. Scrape into
the casserole or pan with the chicken.

COOK'S TIP

If the colour of the sauce seems a little pale,
add 2 – 3 outer leaves of dark green cos lettuce. Cut out the central veins, chop the
leaves and add to the food processor with
the other ingredients. This will lift the
colour without altering the flavour.

4 Make the stock up to 475ml/
16fl oz/2 cups with water, if
necessary. Stir it into the casserole or
pan. Mix gently and simmer just long
enough to blend the flavours and heat
the chicken pieces through. Add salt to
taste. Serve at once, garnished with
coriander and accompanied by rice.

Mole Poblano de Guajolote

Mole Poblano de Guajolote is *the* great festive dish of Mexico. It is served at any special occasion, be it a birthday, wedding, or family get-together. Rice, beans, tortillas and Guacamole are the traditional accompaniments.

INGREDIENTS

Serves 6–8
2.75–3.6kg/6–8lb turkey, cut into
  serving pieces
1 onion, chopped
1 garlic clove, chopped
salt
90ml/6 tbsp lard or corn oil
fresh coriander and 30ml/2 tbsp toasted
  sesame seeds, to garnish

For the sauce
6 dried *ancho* chillies
4 dried *pasilla* chillies
4 dried *mulato* chillies
1 drained canned *chipotle* chilli, seeded
  and chopped (optional)
2 onions, chopped
2 garlic cloves, chopped
450g/1lb tomatoes, peeled
  and chopped
1 stale tortilla, torn into pieces
50g/2oz/⅓ cup seedless raisins
115g/4oz/1 cup ground almonds
45ml/3 tbsp sesame seeds, ground
2.5ml/½ tsp coriander seeds, ground
5ml/1 tsp ground cinnamon
2.5ml/½ tsp ground anise
1.5ml/¼ tsp ground black peppercorns
60ml/4 tbsp lard or corn oil
40g/1½oz unsweetened (bitter)
  chocolate, broken into squares
15ml/1 tbsp sugar
salt and freshly ground pepper

COOK'S TIP

Roasting the dried chillies lightly, taking
care not to burn them, brings out the
flavour and is worth the extra effort.

---

1 Put the turkey pieces into a saucepan or flameproof casserole large enough to hold them in one layer comfortably. Add the onion and garlic, and enough cold water to cover. Season with salt, bring to a gentle simmer, cover and cook for about 1 hour or until the turkey is tender.

2 Meanwhile, put the *ancho, pasilla* and *mulato* chillies in a dry frying pan over gentle heat and roast them for a few minutes, shaking the pan frequently. Remove the stems and shake out the seeds. Tear the pods into pieces and put these into a small bowl. Add sufficient warm water to just cover and soak, turning from time to time, for 30 minutes until soft.

3 Lift out the turkey pieces and pat them dry with kitchen paper. Reserve the stock in a measuring jug. Heat the lard or oil in a large frying pan and sauté the turkey pieces until lightly browned all over. Transfer to a plate and set aside. Reserve the oil that is left in the frying pan.

4 Tip the chillies, with the water in which they have been soaked, into a food processor. Add the *chipotle* chilli, if using, with the onions, garlic, tomatoes, tortilla, raisins, ground almonds and spices. Process to a purée. Do this in batches if necessary.

5 Add the lard or oil to the fat remaining in the frying pan used for sautéing the turkey. Heat the mixture, then add the chilli and spice paste. Cook, stirring, for 5 minutes.

6 Transfer the mixture to the pan or casserole in which the turkey was originally cooked. Stir in 475ml/16fl oz/2 cups of the turkey stock (make it up with water if necessary). Add the chocolate and season with salt and pepper. Cook over a low heat until the chocolate has melted. Stir in the sugar. Add the turkey and more stock if needed. Cover the pan and simmer very gently for 30 minutes. Serve, garnished with fresh coriander and sprinkled with the sesame seeds.

Smoked Beef Tongue with Tomatillos

Tomatillos have a delicious, distinctive flavour and colour.

INGREDIENTS

Serves 6–8

1 smoked ox tongue, about
    2.25kg/5–5¼lb
45ml/3 tbsp corn oil
2 onions, finely chopped
2 garlic cloves, chopped
3 or 4 drained pickled *serrano* or
    jalapeño chillies, seeded and chopped
30ml/2 tbsp chopped fresh coriander
2 x 275g/10oz cans tomatillos
    (Mexican green tomatoes)
salt and freshly ground pepper
fresh coriander, to garnish
small new potatoes, to serve

1 Thoroughly wash the tongue and put it into a large saucepan. Cover with cold water and bring to the boil. Remove any scum that rises to the surface. Lower the heat and simmer, covered, for 3–4 hours until tender. Allow the tongue to cool in the stock.

2 Lift out the tongue when it is cool enough to handle, reserving the stock. Peel the skin from the tongue and trim the root end and discard. Cut the tongue into fairly thick slices and place these in a flameproof casserole.

3 Heat the oil in a large frying pan and sauté the onions and garlic with the chillies until the onion is tender. Add the coriander, the tomatillos (with the can juices) and salt and pepper to taste. Stir to mix and pour over the tongue, adding a little reserved stock if the mixture is thick.

4 Cover the pan with foil or a lid and cook over a moderate heat for about 15 minutes until hot. Serve at once, garnished with coriander sprigs and accompanied by new potatoes sprinkled with chopped coriander.

— COOK'S TIP —

Fresh lamb's tongues can be used – they only need to be cooked for 45–60 minutes.

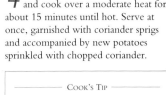

Beef with Cactus Pieces

Nopalitos – chunks of an edible cactus – are used as a vegetable in Mexico, and are the basis of several salads, soups and bakes.

INGREDIENTS

Serves 6

900g/2lb braising beef, cut into
    5cm/2in cubes
30ml/2 tbsp corn oil
1 onion, finely chopped
2 garlic cloves, chopped
1 or 2 *jalapeño* chillies, seeded and
    chopped
115g/4oz can *nopalitos* (cactus pieces),
    rinsed and drained
2 x 275g/10oz tomatillos (Mexican
    green tomatoes)
50g/2oz/½ cup fresh chopped
    coriander
beef stock (optional)
salt and freshly ground black pepper
chopped fresh coriander, to garnish

1 Pat the beef cubes dry with kitchen paper. Heat the oil in a frying pan and sauté the beef cubes a few at a time, until browned all over. Using a slotted spoon, transfer the beef cubes to a flameproof casserole or pan.

2 Add the onion and garlic to the oil remaining in the frying pan and sauté until the onion is tender. Add more oil if necesssary. Add the onions and garlic to the casserole or pan together with the chillies.

3 Add the *nopalitos* and tomatillos, with the can juices, to the casserole. Stir in the coriander until well mixed. If more liquid is needed to cover the beef, stir in as much stock as needed. Season with salt and pepper.

4 Bring to a slow simmer, cover and cook over a low heat for about 2½ hours or until the beef is very tender. Serve sprinkled with the chopped coriander.

COOK'S TIP

Tomatillos (Mexican green tomatoes) are not to be confused with ordinary green unripe tomatoes. Look for them, canned, in speciality markets and food shops.

Lamb Stew

This stew is known as *Estofado de Carnero* in Mexico. The recipe for this dish has an interesting mix of chillies – the mild, full-flavoured *ancho,* and the piquante *jalapeño* which gives extra "bite". The heat of the chillies is mellowed by the additon of ground cinnamon and cloves. Boneless neck fillet is very good for this dish; it is lean, tender, flavoursome and inexpensive.

Ingredients

Serves 4

3 dried *ancho* chillies
30ml/2 tbsp olive oil
1 *jalapeño* chilli, seeded and
  chopped
1 onion, finely chopped
2 garlic cloves, chopped
450g/1lb tomatoes, peeled
  and chopped
50g/2oz/¹/₃ cup seedless raisins
1.5ml/¹/₄ tsp ground cinnamon
1.5ml/¹/₄ tsp ground cloves
900g/2lb boneless lamb, cut into
  5cm/2in cubes
250ml/8fl oz/1 cup lamb stock
  or water
salt and freshly ground black pepper
a few sprigs of fresh coriander,
  to garnish
coriander rice, to serve

1 Roast the *ancho* chillies lightly in a dry frying pan over gentle heat to bring out the flavour.

2 Remove the stems, shake out the seeds and tear the pods into pieces, then put them into a bowl. Pour in enough warm water to just cover. Leave to soak for 30 minutes.

3 Heat the olive oil in a frying pan and sauté the *jalapeño* chilli together with the onion and garlic until the onion is tender.

4 Add the chopped tomatoes to the pan and cook until the mixture is thick and well blended. Stir in the raisins, ground cinnamon and cloves, and season to taste with salt and ground black pepper. Transfer the mixture to a flameproof casserole.

5 Tip the *ancho* chillies and their soaking water into a food processor and process to a smooth purée. Add the chilli pureé to the tomato mixture in the casserole.

6 Add the lamb cubes to the casserole, stir to mix and pour in enough of the lamb stock or water to just cover the meat.

7 Bring to a simmer, then cover the casserole and cook over a low heat for about 2 hours or until the lamb is tender. Garnish with fresh coriander and serve with coriander rice.

COOK'S TIP

To make coriander rice, simply heat 30ml/2 tbsp corn oil in a large frying pan and gently cook 1 finely chopped onion for about 8 minutes or until soft but not brown. Stir in enough cooked, long grain rice for four and stir gently over a very moderate heat until heated through. Sprinkle over 30–45ml/2–3 tbsp chopped fresh coriander and stir in thoroughly.

Meat Balls

Mexican cooks use twice-ground beef and pork for *Albondigas*.

INGREDIENTS

Serves 4

225g/8oz lean minced beef
225g/8oz minced pork
50g/2oz/1 cup fresh white
   breadcrumbs
1 onion, finely chopped
2.5ml/½ tsp dried oregano or
   ground cumin
salt and freshly ground black pepper
1 egg, lightly beaten
milk (optional)
corn oil, for frying
oregano leaves, to garnish

For the sauce

beef stock
1 *chipotle* chilli, seeded and chopped
1 onion, finely chopped
2 garlic cloves, crushed
225g/8oz tomatoes, peeled, seeded and
   finely chopped

1 Put the mixed beef and pork through a mincer or process in a food processor so that the mixture is finely minced. Tip it into a bowl and add the breadcrumbs, onion and oregano or cumin. Season with salt and pepper and stir in the egg.

--- COOK'S TIP ---

The meat balls can be simply poached in beef stock if preferred. Alternatively, you can use fresh tomato sauce or salsa, thinned down as required with beef stock.

2 Knead thoroughly with clean hands to make a smooth mixture, adding a little milk if necessary. Shape the mixture into 4cm/1½in balls.

3 Heat 1cm/½in oil in a frying pan and fry the balls for 5 minutes, turning occasionally, until browned.

4 Put the meat balls into a shallow pan or flameproof casserole and pour over beef stock to cover. Add the remaining ingredients and bring to the boil. Simmer for about 30 minutes. Using a slotted spoon, transfer the meat balls to a serving dish. Press the sauce through a sieve, then spoon it over the meat balls. Serve at once, garnished with oregano leaves.

Pork with Pineapple

INGREDIENTS

Serves 6

30ml/2 tbsp corn oil
900g/2lb boneless pork shoulder or
    loin, cut into 5cm/2in cubes
1 onion, finely chopped
1 large red pepper, seeded and
    finely chopped
1 or more *jalapeño* chillies, seeded and
    finely chopped
450g/1lb fresh pineapple chunks
8 fresh mint leaves, chopped
250ml/8fl oz/1 cup chicken stock
salt and freshly ground black pepper
fresh mint sprig, to garnish
rice, to serve

1 Heat the oil in a large frying pan and sauté the pork in batches until the cubes are lightly coloured. Transfer the pork to a flameproof casserole, leaving the oil behind in the pan.

2 Add the finely chopped onion, finely chopped red pepper and the chilli(es) to the oil remaining in the pan. Sauté until the onion is tender, then add to the casserole with the pineapple. Stir to mix.

3 Add the mint, then cover and simmer gently for about 2 hours, or until the pork is tender. Garnish with fresh mint and serve with rice.

—— COOK'S TIP ——

If fresh pineapple is not available, use pineapple canned in its own juice.

Veal in Nut Sauce

INGREDIENTS

Serves 6

1.5kg/3 – 3½lb boneless veal, cut into
 5cm/2in cubes
2 onions, finely chopped
1 garlic clove, crushed
2.5ml/½tsp dried thyme
2.5ml/½tsp dried oregano
350ml/12fl oz/1½cups chicken stock
75g/3oz/¾ cup very finely ground
 almonds, pecan nuts or peanuts
175g/6fl oz/¾ cup soured cream
fresh oregano, to garnish
rice, to serve

COOK'S TIP

Choose domestically raised pink veal if you
can. It has a much better flavour and tends
to be more moist than white veal.

1 Put the cubes of veal, finely
chopped onions, crushed garlic,
thyme, oregano and chicken stock into
a large flameproof casserole. Bring to a
gentle boil. Cover tightly and simmer
over a low heat for about 2 hours or
until the veal is cooked and tender.

2 Put the ground nuts in a food
processor. Pour in 120ml/4fl oz/
½ cup of the veal liquid and process
for a few seconds until smooth. Press
through a sieve into the casserole.

3 Stir in the soured cream and heat
through gently, without boiling.
Serve at once with rice, if liked.

Picadillo

Serve as a main dish with rice, or
use to stuff peppers or fill tacos.

INGREDIENTS

Serves 6

30ml/2 tbsp olive or corn oil
900g/2lb minced beef
1 onion, finely chopped
2 garlic cloves, chopped
2 eating apples
450g/1lb tomatoes, peeled, seeded and
 chopped
2 or 3 drained pickled *jalapeño* chillies,
 seeded and chopped
65g/2½oz/scant ½ cup raisins
1.5ml/¼tsp ground cinnamon
1.5ml/¼tsp ground cumin
salt and freshly ground black pepper
tortilla chips, to serve

To garnish
15g/½oz/1 tbsp butter
25g/1oz/¼ cup slivered almonds

1 Heat the oil in large frying pan and
add the beef, onion and garlic and
fry, stirring from time to time, until the
beef is brown and the onion is tender.

2 Peel, core and chop the apples.
Add them to the pan with all the
remaining ingredients, except the
almonds. Cook, uncovered, for about
20 – 25 minutes, stirring occasionally.

3 Just before serving, make the
garnish by melting the butter in a
small frying pan and sautéing the
almonds until golden brown. Serve the
Picadillo topped with the almonds and
accompanied by the tortilla chips.

DESSERTS AND PUDDINGS

Until the Conquest, fresh fruit was the principal dessert in Mexico, except for sweet tamales. Once the Spanish arrived, bringing with them wheat flour, milk, butter, eggs and sugar, the picture changed and cooks made more elaborate desserts and puddings. Some of these combined New and Old World ingredients, while others reflected the Moorish influence in Spanish cuisine. It was the Moors who introduced rice to the Spanish mainland, and with it an enduring favourite, Arroz con Leche, *a rice pudding enriched with raisins, cinnamon, sherry and almonds. Other sweet imports included* flan *(caramel custard) and* buñuelos, *easy-to-make fritters that are absolutely delicious.*

King's Day Bread

January 6, the day the Three Kings brought gifts to the infant Jesus, is a traditional gift-giving day in Mexico, when this iced cake-bread is served.

INGREDIENTS

Serves 8

10ml/2 tsp active dry yeast
120ml/4fl oz/½ cup lukewarm water
275g/10oz/2½ cups plain flour
2.5ml/½ tsp salt
50g/2oz/¼ cup granulated sugar
2 eggs, well beaten
4 egg yolks, lightly beaten
115g/4oz/½ cup unsalted butter, softened
350g/12oz/2 cups mixed chopped crystallized fruit and peel
melted butter, for glazing
175g/6oz/1⅓ cups icing sugar, sifted
30ml/2 tbsp single cream
glacé cherries, halved, to decorate

1 Sprinkle the yeast over the water, stir and leave for about 5 minutes or until the mixture is frothy.

2 Put 150g/5oz/1¼ cups of the flour in a bowl. Add the salt, sugar, eggs, egg yolks, butter and yeast. Mix well. Put 225g/8oz/1¼ cups of the crystallized fruit and peel and 50g/2oz/¼ cup of the flour into a bowl and toss to coat. Add to the yeast mixture with the rest of the flour. Beat well to make a soft but not sticky dough.

3 Turn the dough on to a lightly-floured board. Knead until smooth.

4 Shape the dough into a ring, place on a greased baking sheet, cover lightly with a cloth and leave in a warm, draft-free place for up to 2 hours or until it has doubled in size.

5 Preheat the oven to 180°C/350°F/ Gas 4. Brush the ring with melted butter and bake for 30 minutes. Remove from the oven and cool.

6 In a bowl, mix the icing sugar with the cream. Drizzle the icing over the ring. Decorate with the remaining crystallized fruit and peel and the glacé cherries.

Almond Biscuits

INGREDIENTS

Makes about 24

115g/4oz/1 cup plain flour, sifted
175g/6oz/1⅓ cups icing sugar
1.5ml/¼ tsp salt
50g/2oz/½ cup almonds, finely
   chopped
2.5ml/½ tsp vanilla essence
115g/4oz/½ cup unsalted butter,
   softened
icing sugar, for dusting

COOK'S TIP

The biscuits can be varied by using other nuts such as walnuts, peanuts or pecan nuts, or by adding spices of your choice.

1 Preheat the oven to 180°C/350°F/ Gas 4. Combine the flour, icing sugar, salt and almonds in a bowl, mixing well. Stir in the vanilla essence.

2 Using your fingertips, work the butter into the mixture to make a dough. Form it into a ball.

3 Roll out the dough on a lightly floured surface to a thickness of 3mm/⅛in. Using a round cutter, stamp out into about 24 biscuits, re-rolling the trimmings as necessary.

4 Transfer the biscuits to baking sheets and bake for 30 minutes or until they are delicately browned.

5 Cool on wire racks and dust thickly with icing sugar. Store the biscuits in a tightly closed tin or jar.

Churros

INGREDIENTS

Makes about 24
250ml/8fl oz/1 cup water
15ml/1 tbsp granulated sugar, plus
   extra for dusting
2.5ml/½ tsp salt
175g/6oz/1½ cups plain flour
1 large egg
½ lime or lemon
oil for frying

COOK'S TIP

You can use a funnel to shape the churros.
Close the end with a finger, add the batter,
then release into the oil in small columns.

1 Bring the water, sugar and salt to
the boil. Remove from the heat
and beat in the flour until smooth.

2 Beat in the egg, using a wooden
spoon, until the mixture is smooth
and satiny. Set the batter aside.

3 Pour the oil into a deep-frying pan
to a depth of about 5cm/2in. Add
the lime or lemon half, then heat the
oil to 190°C/375°F or until a cube of
day-old bread added to the oil browns
in 30–60 seconds.

4 Pour the batter into a pastry bag
fitted with a fluted nozzle. Pipe
7.5cm/3in strips of batter and then add
to the oil, a few at a time. Fry for
3–4 minutes or until golden brown.

5 Using a slotted spoon, remove the
churros from the pan and drain on
kitchen paper. Roll the hot churros in
granulated sugar before serving.

Sopaipillas

INGREDIENTS

Makes about 30
225g/8oz/2 cups plain flour, sifted
15ml/1 tbsp baking powder
5ml/1 tsp salt
30ml/2 tbsp lard or margarine
175ml/6fl oz/¾ cup water
corn oil, for deep frying
syrup or honey, to serve

COOK'S TIP

Use your imagination when deciding what
to serve with the puffs. Sprinkle them with
cinnamon and sugar, or flavour syrup with
rum. The fat little pillows could even be
served plain, as they taste delicious.

1 Put the flour, baking powder and
salt into a large bowl. Lightly rub
in the lard or margarine, using your
fingertips, until the mixture resembles
coarse breadcrumbs.

2 Gradually stir in the water, using a
fork, until the mixture clumps
together to form a soft dough.

3 Shape the dough into a ball, then
turn out on to a lightly floured
surface and knead very gently until
smooth. Roll out thinly to a rectangle
measuring about 46 x 35cm/18 x 15in.
Using a sharp knife, carefully cut into
about 30 x 7.5cm/3in squares. For a
decorative edge you could use a pastry
wheel to cut out the squares.

4 Heat the oil to 190°C/375°F or
until a cube of day-old bread
browns in 30–60 seconds.

5 Fry the puffs, a few at a time, in
the oil. As they brown and puff
up, turn over to cook the other side.
Remove with a slotted spoon and drain
on kitchen paper. It is important that
the temperature of the oil remains
constant during the cooking process.
Serve warm, with syrup or honey or
any sauce of your choice.

Caramel Custard

This is a classic dessert in Mexico where it is known simply as *flan*.

INGREDIENTS

Serves 6

275g/10oz/1¼ cups granulated sugar
1 litre/1¾ pints/4 cups milk
6 eggs, lightly beaten
5ml/1 tsp vanilla essence
pinch of salt

1 Preheat the oven to 180°C/350°F/ Gas 4. To make the caramel, put 115g/4oz/½ cup of the sugar into a small heavy-based saucepan. Heat, stirring constantly, until the sugar melts. Warm six ramekins by rinsing them in hot water and drying them quickly. Continue to heat the sugar syrup, without stirring, until it turns a deep golden colour. Remove the pan from the heat.

2 Pour some of the caramel into a ramekin and turn it so it coats the bottom and sides. As soon as the caramel sets, turn the ramekin upside down on a baking sheet. Coat the remaining ramekins in the same way.

--- COOK'S TIP ---

Vary the flavour by adding a little ground cinnamon, cocoa or rum instead of vanilla.

3 Scald the milk by heating it in a saucepan to just below boiling point. Pour into a jug and cool.

4 Put the eggs into a bowl and gradually beat in the remaining sugar. Add the cooled milk, vanilla essence and salt. Mix together well.

5 Strain the egg mixture into the ramekins and put them into a roasting tin filled with enough hot water to come halfway up the sides of the ramekins.

6 Bake for about 40 minutes or until a knife inserted in the centre of the custard comes out clean.

7 Cool the custards, then chill for several hours in the fridge.

8 Wet a non-serrated knife and run it between the custard and the side of the ramekin. Put a plate upside down over the ramekin and invert it quickly. The flan will easily slide out.

Rice Pudding

Rice pudding is popular the world over and is always different. This version – *Arroz con Leche* – is light and attractive and very easy to make.

INGREDIENTS

Serves 4

75g/3oz/½ cup raisins
90g/3½ oz/½ cup short grain rice
2.5cm/1in strip of lime or lemon peel
250ml/8fl oz/1 cup water
475ml/16fl oz/2 cups milk
225g/8oz/1 cup granulated sugar
1.5ml/¼ tsp salt
2.5cm/1in cinnamon stick
2 egg yolks, well beaten
15g/½ oz/1 tbsp unsalted
    butter, cubed
toasted flaked almonds to decorate
segments of fresh peeled oranges,
    to serve

COOK'S TIP

It is essential to use short grain rice for this pudding. Short grain is sometimes packaged with the name "pudding rice".

1 Put the raisins into a small bowl. Cover with warm water and set aside to soak. Put the short grain rice into a saucepan together with the lime or lemon peel and water. Bring slowly to the boil and then lower the heat. Cover the pan and simmer very gently for about 20 minutes or until all the water has been absorbed.

2 Remove the peel from the rice and discard it. Add the milk, sugar, salt and cinnamon and cook, stirring, over a very low heat until all the milk has been absorbed. Do not cover the pan.

3 Discard the cinnamon stick. Add the egg yolks and cubed butter, stirring constantly until the butter has melted and the pudding is rich and creamy. Drain the raisins well and stir them into the rice. Cook the pudding for a few minutes longer.

4 Tip the rice into a dish and cool. Serve with the orange segments, decorated with the almonds.

Pumpkin in Brown Sugar

Ingredients

Serves 4

900g/2lb pumpkin, cut into wedges
350g/12oz/2 cups soft dark
   brown sugar
about 120ml/4fl oz/½ cup water

1 Scrape the seeds out of the pumpkin wedges. Pack the wedges firmly together in a heavy-based flameproof casserole.

2 Divide the sugar among the pumpkin pieces, packing it into the hollows which contained the seeds.

— Cook's Tip —

The best pumpkin for this recipe is the classic orange-fleshed variety used to make Hallowe'en lanterns. Choose one which will fit neatly into your casserole when cut.

3 Pour the water carefully into the casserole to cover the bottom and prevent the pumpkin from burning. Take care not to dislodge the sugar when pouring in the water.

4 Cover and cook over a low heat, checking the water level frequently, until the pumpkin is tender and the sugar has dissolved in the liquid to form a sauce.

5 Using a slotted spoon, transfer the pumpkin to a serving dish. Pour the sugary liquid from the pan over the pumpkin and serve at once with natural yogurt, sweetened with a little brown sugar, if you like.

Buñuelos

INGREDIENTS

Serves 6

225g/8oz/2 cups plain flour
5ml/1 tsp baking powder
2.5ml/½ tsp salt
15ml/1 tbsp granulated sugar
1 large egg, beaten
120ml/4fl oz/½ cup milk
25g/1oz/2 tbsp unsalted butter, melted
oil, for frying
sugar, for dusting

For the syrup

225g/8oz/1⅓ cups soft light
   brown sugar
750ml/1¼ pints/3 cups water
2.5cm/1in cinnamon stick
1 clove

1 Make the syrup. Combine all the ingredients in a saucepan. Heat, stirring, until the sugar has dissolved, then simmer until the mixture has reduced to a light syrup. Remove and discard the spices. Keep the syrup warm while you make the *buñuelos*.

2 Sift the flour, salt and baking powder into a bowl. Stir in the sugar. In a mixing bowl, whisk the egg and the milk well together. Gradually stir in the dry mixture, then beat in the melted butter to make a soft dough.

3 Turn the dough on to a lightly floured board and knead until it is smooth and elastic. Divide the dough into 18 even-size pieces. Shape into balls. With your hands, flatten the balls to disk shapes about 2cm/¾in thick.

4 Use the floured handle of a wooden spoon to poke a hole through the centre of each *buñuelo*. Pour oil into a deep frying pan to a depth of 5cm/2in. Alternatively, use a deep-fryer. Heat the oil to a temperature of 190°C/375°F or until a cube of day-old bread added to the oil browns in 30–60 seconds.

5 Fry the fritters in batches, taking care not to overcrowd the pan, until they are puffy and golden brown on both sides. Lift out with a slotted spoon and drain on kitchen paper.

6 Dust the *buñuelos* with sugar and serve with the syrup.

Almond Pudding with Custard

INGREDIENTS

Serves 6 – 8

250ml/8fl oz/1 cup water
1 sachet powdered gelatine
225g/8oz/1 cup granulated sugar
2.5ml/½tsp almond essence
6 egg whites
ground cinnamon, for dusting

For the custard

6 egg yolks
50g/2oz/¼ cup granulated sugar
pinch of salt
475ml/16fl oz/2 cups single cream
2.5ml/½tsp vanilla essence

1 Pour the water into a saucepan and sprinkle the gelatine over the surface. When it has softened, add the sugar and place the pan over a low heat. Stir until both the gelatine and the sugar have completely dissolved.

2 Stir in the almond essence. Pour the mixture into a bowl, cool, then chill until it begins to thicken.

3 Whisk the egg whites in a grease-free bowl until stiff peaks form.

4 Beat the gelatine mixture until it is frothy, then fold in the egg whites. Turn into a serving bowl and chill for several hours, or until firm.

5 Meanwhile, make the custard. Mix the egg yolks, sugar and salt in a double boiler or heavy-based saucepan. Add the cream and cook over a very low heat, stirring constantly, until the custard coats the spoon.

6 Remove the custard from the heat and stir in the vanilla essence. Cover the surface of the custard with dampened greaseproof paper to prevent the formation of a skin. Cool, then chill. Serve with the pudding, dusted with cinnamon, if you like.

COOK'S TIP

As soon as the custard coats the spoon remove it from the heat as the custard will thin out if cooked beyond this point.

Coconut Custard

INGREDIENTS

Serves 6

225g/8oz/1 cup granulated sugar
250ml/8fl oz/1 cup water
7.5cm/3in cinnamon stick
115g/4oz/1 cup grated fresh coconut
750ml/1¼pints/3 cups milk
4 eggs
175ml/6fl oz/³/₄ cup whipping cream
475ml/3 tbsp toasted chopped
   almonds (optional)

1 Combine the sugar, water and cinnamon stick in a large saucepan. Bring to the boil, then lower the heat and simmer, uncovered, for 5 minutes. Remove the cinnamon stick.

2 Add the grated coconut to the pan, and cook over a low heat for 5 minutes more. Stir in the milk and cook, stirring from time to time, until the mixture has thickened to the consistency of thin custard. Remove from the heat and set aside.

3 Beat the eggs in a bowl until fluffy. Add a ladleful (about 45ml/3 tbsp) of the coconut mixture to the eggs and stir to mix. Continue to add the coconut mixture in this way, then return the contents of the bowl to the clean pan. Stir well.

4 Cook over a low heat, stirring constantly with a wooden spoon until the mixture becomes a thick custard. Pour into a serving dish.

5 Cool the custard, then chill until ready to serve. Whip the cream until thick and spread it over the custard. Decorate with the toasted chopped almonds, if using.

> —————— COOK'S TIP ——————
>
> The easiest way to prepare a fresh coconut is to bake it in a preheated 180°C/350°F/ Gas 4 oven for 15 minutes, then pierce two of the eyes with an icepick or sharp skewer and drain out the milk. Open the coconut by hitting it carefully with a hammer; it will break into several pieces, making it easy to remove the shell. Peel off the brown skin, chop the flesh into small pieces and grate in a food processor.

DRINKS

Mexicans slake their thirst with a wide range of beverages, from the ancient corn drink atole *right through to the modern tequila cocktail, the Margarita.* Refrescos – *fruit drinks of various kinds – are very popular, as are beers, wines, liqueurs, rum and other tequila-based cocktails. Mexico is coffee and chocolate country and these beverages are prepared in a unique fashion. Some fruit drinks feature flowers, as when hibiscus sepals are used to make* Agua de Jamaica. Agua de Tamarindo *is made with tamarind pulp and there are many other unusual and exotic drinks to discover in this fascinating country.*

Sangrita

INGREDIENTS

Serves 8

450g/1lb tomatoes, peeled, seeded
   and chopped
120ml/4fl oz/½ cup orange juice
60ml/4 tbsp freshly squeezed lime juice
1 small onion, chopped
2.5ml/½ tsp granulated sugar
6 small fresh green chillies, seeded
   and chopped
salt
50ml/2oz aged tequila (*Tequila Añejo*)
   per person

COOK'S TIP

Plain white tequila is not suitable for this.
Choose one of the amber aged tequilas
(*Añejos*), which are smoother and more
gentle on the palate.

1 Put the chopped tomatoes, orange
juice, lime juice, chopped onion,
granulated sugar and chopped green
chillies into a food processor.

2 Process the tomato mixture until
very smooth, scraping down the
sides if necessary.

3 Pour the tomato mixture into a jug
and chill well.

4 To serve, pour into small glasses,
allowing about 90ml/6 tbsp per
portion. Pour the tequila into separate
small glasses. Sip the tomato juice and
tequila alternately.

Sangria

This very popular summer drink
was borrowed from Spain. The
Mexican version is slightly less
alcoholic than the original.

INGREDIENTS

Serves 6

ice cubes
1 litre/1¾ pints/4 cups dry red
   table wine
150ml/¼ pint/⅔ cup freshly squeezed
   orange juice
50ml/2fl oz/¼ cup freshly squeezed
   lime juice
115g/4oz/½ cup caster sugar
2 limes or 1 apple, sliced, to serve

1 Half fill a large jug with ice cubes.
Pour in the wine and the orange
and lime juices.

2 Add the sugar and stir well until it
has dissolved. Pour into tumblers
and float the lime or apple slices on
top. Serve at once.

COOK'S TIP

Sugar does not dissolve readily in alcohol. I
prefer to use simple syrup, which is very
easy to make and gives a smoother drink.
Combine 450g/1lb/2 cups granulated sugar
and 475ml/16fl oz/2 cups water in a jug and
set aside until the sugar has dissolved. Stir
from time to time. 15ml/1 tbsp simple syrup
is the equivalent of 7.5ml/1½ tsp sugar.

Rompope

This drink could best be described as cooked eggnog. It keeps well if chilled but seldom gets the chance.

INGREDIENTS

Makes about 1.75 litres/3 pints/7½ cups
1 litre/1¾ pints/4 cups milk
225g/8oz/1 cup granulated sugar
5cm/2in cinnamon stick
50g/2oz/½ cup ground almonds
12 large egg yolks
475ml/16fl oz/2 cups medium rum

───── COOK'S TIP ─────

Try serving this over lots of ice in a tall tumbler for a deliciously long drink.

1 Combine the milk, sugar and cinnamon in a large saucepan. Simmer over a very low heat, stirring constantly, until the sugar has dissolved.

2 Cool to room temperature. Remove the cinnamon stick and stir in the ground almonds.

3 Beat the egg yolks in a bowl until they are very thick and pale.

4 Add the egg yolks to the almond mixture a little at a time, beating well. Return the pan to the heat and cook gently until the mixture coats a spoon. Cool.

5 Stir in the rum. Pour into a clean dry bottle and cork tightly. Keep in the fridge for 2 days before serving as an aperitif or liqueur.

Tequila Cocktail

The traditional way to drink tequila is to place some salt on the back of the left hand between the base of the thumb and index finger. Taking care not to spill the salt, hold a halved lime in the same hand. Then hold a small tequila glass in the right hand. Lick a little salt, down the tequila and immediately suck the lime.

INGREDIENTS

Serves 2
100ml/3½fl oz/scant ½ cup white tequila
90ml/6 tbsp freshly squeezed lime juice
30ml/2 tbsp grenadine syrup
crushed ice
twists of lime rind, to serve

1 Combine the tequila, lime juice and grenadine syrup in a mixing glass and stir to mix thoroughly.

2 Three-quarters fill two cocktail glasses with crushed ice and carefully pour the tequila cocktail mixture into each glass. Serve each drink with one or two short drinking straws and a twist of lime rind.

Bloody Maria

Ingredients

Serves 2

175ml/6fl oz/³/₄ cup tomato juice
90ml/3fl oz/6 tbsp white tequila
dash each of Worcestershire and
    Tabasco sauces
30ml/2 tbsp lemon juice
salt and freshly ground black pepper
8 ice cubes

───── Cook's Tip ─────

When drinks are to be served with ice,
make sure all the ingredients are thoroughly chilled ahead of time.

1 Combine the tomato juice, tequila, Worcestershire and Tabasco sauces, and lemon juice in a cocktail shaker. Add salt and pepper to taste, and four ice cubes. Shake very vigorously.

2 Place the remaining ice cubes in two heavy-based tumblers and strain the tequila over them.

Margarita

Tequila is made from the sap of a fleshy-leafed plant called the blue agave and gets its name from the town of Tequila, where it has been made for more than 200 years. The Margarita is the most popular and well-known drink made with tequila.

Ingredients

Serves 2

¹/₂ lime or lemon
salt
120ml/4fl oz/¹/₂ cup white tequila
30ml/2 tbsp Triple Sec or Cointreau
30ml/2 tbsp freshly squeezed lime or
    lemon juice
4 or more ice cubes

───── Cook's Tip ─────

It really is worth going to the trouble of buying limes for this recipe. Lemons will do, but something of the special flavour of the drink will be lost in the substitution.

1 Rub the rims of two cocktail glasses with the lime or lemon. Pour some salt into a saucer and dip in the glasses so that the rims are frosted.

2 Combine the tequila, Triple Sec or Cointreau, and lime and lemon juice in a jug and stir to mix well.

3 Pour the tequila mixture into the prepared glasses. Add the ice cubes and serve at once.

Pot Coffee

In Mexico *Cafe de Olla* is made with the local Mexican brown sugar, known as *piloncillo*. Soft dark brown sugar can be used and makes a fine substitute.

INGREDIENTS

Serves 4

1 litre/1¾ pints/4 cups water
115g/4oz/²⁄₃ cup soft dark brown sugar
5cm/2in cinnamon stick
3 cloves
50g/2oz/²⁄₃ cup medium ground dark
   roasted coffee

1 Combine the water, soft brown sugar, cinnamon stick and cloves in a saucepan. Slowly bring to the boil over a low heat. Stir occasionally until the sugar has dissolved completely.

2 Stir in the ground coffee and boil for 1 minute more. Remove from the heat, cover and leave to steep for about 5 minutes.

3 Strain the coffee through a fine sieve into small cups or mugs. Serve immediately.

Corn Drink with Milk

In Aztec times this drink – *Atole de Leche* – would have been made with plain water as milk was not available until the Spanish introduced cattle. It would have been sweetened with honey, or not sweetened at all, as sugar was another ingredient introduced by the Conquerors.

INGREDIENTS

Serves 6

50g/2oz/½ cup *masa harina*
   (tortilla flour)
475ml/16fl oz/2 cups water
1 vanilla pod
1 litre/1¾ pints/4 cups milk
a little granulated sugar

1 Combine the *masa harina* and the water in a large heavy-based saucepan, stirring to mix well. Add the vanilla pod and cook over a low heat, stirring constantly, until the mixture has thickened.

2 Remove the pan from the heat and gradually stir in the milk. Sweeten with granulated sugar to taste.

3 Return the pan to the heat and cook for just long enough to heat through, stirring all the time. Remove the vanilla pod and serve the drink hot.

Chocolate Corn Drink

In Mexico, drinking chocolate is beaten with a very pretty carved wooden *molinillo*, but a wire whisk does the job just as well if not so decoratively. This traditional drink also contains *masa harina* and is known in Mexico as *Champurrado*.

INGREDIENTS

Serves 6
50g/2oz/½ cup *masa harina*
    (tortilla flour)
750ml/1¼ pints/3 cups plain water
5cm/2in cinnamon stick
750ml/1¼ pints/3 cups milk
75g/3oz/3 squares Mexican chocolate,
    or any unsweetened (bitter)
    chocolate, grated
a little soft light brown sugar

1 Combine the *masa harina* and water in a large saucepan, stirring to mix well. Add the cinnamon stick and cook, stirring, over a low heat until the mixture has thickened.

2 Gradually stir in the milk, then the grated chocolate. Continue to cook until all the chocolate has dissolved, beating with a whisk or a Mexican *molinollo*. Discard the cinnamon stick. Sweeten to taste with brown sugar. Serve hot in cups.

COOK'S TIP

If Mexican chocolate isn't available, use unsweetened (bitter) chocolate instead.

Mexican Hot Chocolate

INGREDIENTS

Serves 1
250ml/8fl oz/1 cup water or milk or
    a mixture
40g/1½ oz Mexican chocolate or any
    unsweetened (bitter) chocolate

1 Put the water or milk in a saucepan together with the chocolate and slowly bring to a simmer over a low heat. Simmer, stirring continuously, until the chocolate has melted. Continue to heat gently for 4–5 minutes to blend the flavours.

2 Pour the chocolate into a jug and beat with a *molinillo* (see above) until frothy. If a *molinillo* is not available, use a whisk or an electric mixer. Pour the chocolate into a mug and serve at once.

Rosella Drink

In Mexico, the bright red sepals of a tropical flowering plant, *Hibiscus sabdariffa*, are used to make drinks. Available fresh in the Caribbean at Christmas and dried at other times, the plant is known in Mexico as *Flor de Jamaica* and elsewhere as rosella and sorrel. This drink is known as *Agua de Jamaica*.

INGREDIENTS

Serves 4
1 litre/1³/₄ pints/4 cups water
50g/2oz rosella sepals
a little granulated sugar

─── COOK'S TIP ───

This soft drink can be made very festive with the addition of light rum. Mix 50ml/2fl oz light rum with an equal amount of Rosella Drink per serving.

1 Combine the water and rosella sepals in a large saucepan. Bring to the boil over a moderate heat.

2 Allow to boil gently, uncovered, for 1 minute, then remove from the heat and leave to stand for 15 minutes. Stir in a little sugar to sweeten. Strain into a jug. Cool, then cover and chill very well.

3 Serve the ice-cold Rosella Drink in long tumblers filled with ice.

Tamarind Drink

INGREDIENTS

Serves 4
225g/8oz tamarind pods
1 litre/1³/₄ pints/4 cups water
a little granulated sugar

─── COOK'S TIP ───

Tamarind pulp is sometimes sold in tropical markets and Indian or Oriental stores. Using it saves the trouble of peeling the pods, but will still require soaking and sieving, as described below.

1 Peel the tamarind pods and put them into a saucepan. Pour in the water and leave to soak for 4 hours.

2 Mash the tamarind pulp thoroughly with a fork and remove and discard the seeds. Press the pulp through a sieve into a large bowl.

3 Sweeten the *Agua de Tamarindo* to taste. Pour into a jug and chill. Serve in long tumblers filled with ice.

Index